W9-AIB-252

Hidden Treasures

Millie Young

with Sandee Lee

One Mission Society

Greenwood, Indiana

By God's grace, One Mission Society unites, inspires and equips Christians to make disciples of Jesus Christ, multiplying dynamic communities of believers around the world.

One Mission Society is an evangelical, interdenominational faith mission that makes disciples of Jesus Christ through intentional evangelism, planting churches and training national leaders in Africa, Asia, the Caribbean, Europe and Latin America. OMS then joins with those churches in global partnerships to reach the rest of the world.

One Mission Society
PO Box A
Greenwood, IN 46142
317.888.3333
www.onemissionsociety.org

Cover design by W. Foster Pilcher.

Printed in the United States of America

CONTENTS

Acknowledgements 3

1 He Keeps the Keys 7

2 No Impossibilities With God 11

3 Planting the Seed 19

4 Hiding God's Word 25

5 Do Not Move Another Inch 31

6 Broken and Spilled Out 37

7 Making a Change 43

8 Hidden Treasure 49

9 On Fire 57

10 In the Line of Duty 63

11 Victory in Spite of Evil 75

12 Nothing Will Harm You 81

13 Stop. Drop. Pray. 85

14 First Love 95

15 God Will Provide 101

16 A Romance Begins 105

17 A Dream Come True 115

18 Smiling at the Storm 127

19 Sowing With Tears 133

20 Wading Through the Waters 137

21 Time Is Short 145

22 Saying Goodbye 153

23 None of These Things Move Me 167

24 On Stage 173
25 Prayer Changes 179
26 I Signed Up for This 183
27 Against All Odds 195
28 Present Your Requests to God 203
29 Not in Vain 211
Epilogue 217

Acknowledgments

Hidden Treasures relates some of my experiences of uncovering treasures in Colombia, South America. Over the years, God revealed many beautiful people that I grew to recognize as priceless jewels while I worked spreading the message of God's salvation.

I would like to thank Sandee Lee for her encouragement and excitement as she guided me in organizing my experiences and in writing *Hidden Treasures*. I appreciate all the time and energy she put into making this book possible. I would also like to thank her husband Raymond for his patience, kindness, and encouragement.

Amy Ragland has my gratitude for doing the initial edit of this book. Her corrections and suggestions were invaluable.

At OMS headquarters, I would like to thank Susan Loobie who, from the very start, greatly encouraged me to put my experiences in Colombia into writing. A special thank you goes to Lori McFall for the hours she gave to the final editing of the book. For his skill with the design of the book cover, I thank Foster Pilcher.

Mildred (Millie) Young

*****

What a privilege to work side-by-side with such a humble, inspiring woman. I am grateful to Millie for asking me to work with her on this project. I grew spiritually during our many hours of conversation.

Sandee Lee

CHAPTER ONE

He Keeps the Keys
My Call to Colombia

"The LORD is good to those whose hope is in him, to the
one who seeks him." Lamentations 3:25

*****

Millie's insight: We often make our plans, but they are not always God's. Those times of waiting teach us valuable
lessons to serve him better.

*****

During my childhood, many times my father said to me, "Pete,
you would argue with a fence post!" Well, when I believed
something was right, I was determined to stay by it. But becoming a missionary to Colombia, South America, was going to take
more than determination. I needed to have real assurance from
the heavenly Father that Colombia was truly where he was calling me.

Could I, as a young, upstart college graduate really believe
that I was going to enter the country of Colombia, South
America as a missionary? Colombia had closed its doors to
Protestant missionaries in 1948 and exhibited brutal opposition
to any Gospel undertaking within its borders. Did I correctly
understand God's calling for me to go there?

As I sought God's direction, he led me to Proverbs 3:5–6. "Trust in the Lord with all your heart and lean not on your own understanding; in all your ways acknowledge him and he will make your paths straight." So that is what I did. My faith and reliance on God would give me strength to meet whatever challenge was placed before me.

I was sure God was calling me to the mission field in Colombia. Colombia is a Catholic country. At that time, the Catholic Church had total control of the school system and much of the government. They exerted dictatorial power, and as is too often true of organizations developed by man, the Catholic organization had lost its spiritual roots as it became all-powerful. Many atrocities were perpetuated against anyone who did not conform to its expectations. Any state church has the potential to be used by Satan and ceases to be God's vehicle. Too often, power corrupts man and his institutions. The Catholic Church in Colombia, its practices and its influence, has evolved over the years. Because lay people are now permitted to read the Bible, in recent years, changes in the Catholic Church in Colombia have resulted in the Gospel of salvation being preached. Today, many of the Colombian Catholic Churches are preaching the Gospel rather than a message of control and hate.

After graduating from Friends University in Wichita, Kansas, I taught first grade for a year in Towanda, Kansas, which is a small town just a few miles northeast of Wichita. I knew this would be a temporary job during the time I was making plans to be a missionary. God led me to apply to The Oriental Missionary Society (OMS). This organization later changed its name to One Mission Society. When I received a phone call from OMS in March 1954, accepting my application to be a teacher for missionary children in Medellín, Colombia, I submitted my resignation to the school board in Towanda to be effective at the end of that school year.

God led me to the Christians who were willing to support me in my missionary efforts. August 28, 1954, I excitedly headed to language school in Costa Rica. Since my assignment was to teach in English, the mission granted me only four months to study Spanish. However, because my visa to enter

Colombia was denied several times, I continued studying Spanish at language school for 13 months. The denial of my visa, although frustrating at the time, was all part of God's plan as I became more fluent in Spanish. This improved fluency proved to be invaluable later.

While I was waiting for my visa, I began to question if I had correctly understood God's direction. Had I been mistaken? Then God spoke to me through the writing of Mrs. Charles E. Cowman. I was reading her devotional book *Streams in the Desert* during my personal quiet time with God. The January 10 devotion included a poem by an anonymous writer. That poem, especially the verses below, is what God used to encourage me.

Is there some door closed by the Father's hand
    Which widely opened you had hoped to see?
Trust God and wait—for when He shuts the door
    He keeps the key.

Unfailing comfort, sweet and blessed rest,
    To know of EVERY door He keeps the key.
That He at last when just HE sees 'tis best,
    Will give it THEE.[1]

Sometimes, God gives us side excursions. After language school, OMS sent me to Ecuador on a temporary assignment while they continued to work on obtaining a Colombian visa for me. After three months in Ecuador, just as I was starting to fall in love with the Ecuadorian people, I received word that my Colombian visa had been approved.

I was a bit frightened as I flew into Cali, Colombia, because I had no idea how the Colombian officials would treat me. Getting my visa had been such a long, difficult process. But at the same time, I was confident because I knew that God had taken his key to that door and given it to me.

My visa said I was being admitted into Colombia to teach English-speaking children, which is what the telegram to the consulate in Ecuador said. But the Colombian consulate in Ecuador hand-wrote on my passport that I was to teach only in the George Washington School in Medellín. OMS operated this school to educate the children of the English-speaking missionary community. Children of missionaries that represented several different mission societies were admitted to the school.

I was determined to reach the Colombian children and was not going to be deterred. I faithfully followed the directions on my visa. I gladly taught the English-speaking children at George Washington School in Medellín five days a week when school was in session. I joyfully completed the work the Colombian officials stated that I was to do on that first passport.

But my heart was for all children—not just English-speaking children. And what was I to do with all of my spare time? I had no responsibilities on Saturdays, Sundays, or during the summer months. I decided it would not violate my visa if I were to do volunteer work during the hours I was not fulfilling my teaching responsibilities. Besides, I knew that I would forget the Spanish I had worked so hard for 13 months to learn if I did not use it frequently and communicate with native speakers. So I devised a plan. I would tell Bible stories and evangelize children in a poor area not far from the mission compound. Once the plan was hatched, I hopped right into it.

And that was the way I approached my activities as a missionary. I listened to God during my prayer time, and then I looked for the opportunities he was placing before me. Once I knew God's directions, I started enthusiastically spreading the salvation message by working with the Colombian children. They are what I describe as hidden treasures. It was a great joy to find those hidden treasures and then to work with them as they grew in their faith and spread the Gospel message in the cities and through the rural areas of Colombia.

*****

Millie's insight: In our quiet time with God, he directs our paths, and we must patiently wait and trust his leading.

CHAPTER TWO

No Impossibilities With God

"For nothing is impossible with God." Luke 1:37

*****

Millie's insight: God has a plan for every person placed on this earth. It is our responsibility to be wise, humble, and open to his guiding. God will bring his plan to fruition. It will not matter where, under what conditions, or what circumstances we are born.

*****

I was nestled in a box behind the wood cook stove. At birth, I weighed only three and one-half pounds, and no one expected me to live. Even though it was a hot June day, my parents, Howard and Melita McCary, had placed me close to the wood-burning cookstove, hoping the extra warmth would help keep me alive. Infant incubators were not to be found in rural northwest Arkansas.

Life on the rocky farmland was not easy, but we were a happy family. I remember learning about Abraham living in a tent with the Hebrew people. Many nights during the hot summers, quilts were spread on the ground as sleeping in the log cabin was uncomfortably hot. We would look up at the sky, much as Abraham must have done each night in the desert. I would try to count the stars as I fell asleep.

During my high school and college days, most people thought I was a very timid person. However, God had embedded in me the strong faith of my precious mother. Mother believed she was to "… fan into flame the gift of God"[1] like Paul admonished his young protégé Timothy. God had given me strength that was not readily evident to people who did not know me well. It was a strength that compelled me to the mission field shortly after I graduated from college. As the leaders of OMS laid their hands upon me at the annual OMS convention in Winona Lake, Indiana, in the summer of 1954 just before my departure, I was reminded of the strength God had promised to those who believe. Paul taught, "For God did not give us a spirit of timidity, but a spirit of power, of love and of self-discipline."[2] God miraculously had changed my natural timidity into a spirit of power, love, and self-discipline.

It was no surprise to God that in my early twenties I was boarding a plane in Chicago, Illinois, for San Jose, Costa Rica. It was my first plane ride and the first time to be away from family for more than a few days. I was traveling by myself, and doubts crept into my mind. Would I survive four years without seeing my parents and siblings? Was God really calling me to Colombia, South America? Colombia did not welcome evangelical missionaries into their country. It seemed like an impossible situation. But I knew God was calling me, so I went. I knew God has the key to every door we encounter in life. He can open or close it, and no man can undo what God locks or opens.

Over the loud speaker came the announcement to board the flight for San Jose, Costa Rica. Mother and I tightly hugged each other. As tears flowed down our checks, Mother said, "I am happy to see you go to serve the Lord, but it is hard to see you go alone. Yet I know that you are not alone. God is with you."

I arrived at language school not knowing one single word of Spanish. The fact that I would need to study hard did not worry me for I was a good student. However, as I soon found out, the

Spanish language was only a small part of what I would learn in Costa Rica.

I was housed in a dorm room just across the road from the language institute with several other gals. We had a maid. What a different style of living that was! Without any input from me, my roommates chose me to be in charge of the meals when the maid was off duty. I was never a gourmet cook, but I was not afraid to step up and do what was needed. The maid was patient with my poor Spanish skills as she taught me how to prepare Costa Rican dishes. I loved the cooking lessons and the opportunity to practice speaking the few Spanish words I had learned.

The original OMS proposal was for me to do four months of language study in San Jose and then settle in Colombia as a teacher for the children of missionary families. However, I soon learned that God had another plan altogether. Learning Spanish proved to be harder than I thought it would be. My time in language school extended to 13 months.

Language school was not just a place for learning Spanish. We learned the culture of the Latin American countries. Understanding the culture was essential to successful evangelical missionary work. To become one of them, you had to be willing to live among the local people and share their way of life.

Many times, my friends and I attended early Spanish service at the local church. Going to church where you cannot understand what is being said can be discouraging, but it was a good way to listen to native Spanish speakers. After attending service at the Spanish-speaking church, we would go to the English-speaking church that was nearby. Before long, I found myself desiring to become involved in the children's ministry, so I visited the children's class in the Spanish-speaking church. It broke my heart to see 40 little children crowded into a small space with inadequate materials for the teacher to use as she presented the Bible story. The tithe out of my next support check was used to purchase materials. It increased my desire to learn to speak Spanish well enough to teach the children about God.

One afternoon, a preteen girl from our church appeared at

the dorm. While visiting with her, we learned that she was planning to quit school. Her sewing teacher required the girls to bring material to class to make a dress. That poor girl had neither material nor any money to purchase material, so she had decided to drop out and seek employment. I asked her if the dress had to be for her. She replied that it could be for anyone. I had purchased some material just a few days earlier and cut out dresses for three little girls. I loved to sew, and I knew I could find three girls who would enjoy a new dress. When I brought out the material for one dress, I learned that she had two younger sisters who also had to make dresses as a school assignment. What a blessing to give the fabric I had cut out for the three dresses to that girl. Obviously God knew who needed the dress material and the difference it would make in the lives of those three sisters who would now be able to continue their studies.

A missionary friend had a Good News Club for children in an unreached, needy neighborhood. One afternoon she invited me to accompany her to the class. About two weeks later, my friend asked me to take over her class, as she soon would be leaving Costa Rica. It was my love for children and a desire to see them come to Christ at an early age that had led me into missionary service. Yet I was hesitant. Was my Spanish good enough? I decided to give it my best effort. My first solo class in Spanish was August 14, 1955. I taught the story of the four fishermen whom Jesus called to follow him and he would make them fishers of men. We played little rhythm band instruments, sang songs, colored pictures, and ate the freshly baked cookies I had made for this special occasion.

I received a telegram August 16, 1955, from the lawyer who was working on my papers for the Colombian visa. It said, "Bad news with regard to Senorita McCary. There is some private understanding or behind the scenes scheme evidently that exists and on July 23 a communication directed to the Colombian consul in San Jose forbade him to give Miss McCary a visa, because it was considered to be 'inconvenient'."

I had graduated from the language institute, my Costa Rican visa would expire soon, and my airplane ticket would soon no longer be valid. The decision was made that I would remain in Costa Rica until every possible effort had been made to obtain the visa.

It was a difficult time. I helped my classmates pack their things when they graduated from language school. I even rejoiced with them as they were taking the next step in their missionary journeys. One encouraging thing for me was the Good News Club every Thursday at 4:30 p.m. But I needed something more to occupy my time. I went to the Christian radio station and offered to give them three or four hours in the mornings, doing typing or whatever was needed. Then I arranged for private Spanish lessons five days a week. I needed to continue to improve my ability to communicate. When my little Costa Rican church asked me to take over the primary Sunday school class, I was thrilled.

Even after 13 months, OMS had not been successful in getting my visa to enter Colombia. On August 29, I received word from Colombia that it seemed impossible at this time to get a visa for me because of the political situation. Therefore, OMS made plans for me to go to Ecuador for two or three months. That would give them more time to take steps to get the Colombian visa. It was a difficult time. I was disappointed. Why Ecuador? Why did I have to wait any longer? I was sure God had called me to Colombia.

With my tourist visa in hand, I left Costa Rica on September 12, 1955, for Guayaquil, Ecuador. I was to be teaching in a bilingual school, but it was not a Christian school. However, I was soon to find out there were ample opportunities for me to work in children's ministry under the guidance of Geneva DeYoung, who had started her missionary work in Colombia. The relatively new field for OMS in Ecuador was growing. I grasped the opportunity of working with some well-seasoned missionaries who guided and trained me in the practical aspects of developing mission work. Besides teaching at the bilingual school, I worked in children's ministry, women's Bible studies, youth ministries, and made visits to the tuberculosis sanitarium. I was joyfully engaged in ministry.

Guayaquil is a seaport town. The marketplace reeked with smells that just can't be described. During my first trip to the market, I asked our field director to buy the meat because the odor was overwhelming. I stepped into the open so I would not faint on him. Before long, I could do my own shopping as I became more accustomed to the town's sights and smells. The three months of my planned stay swept by rapidly because I fell in love with the Ecuadorian people. They had become a part of my life.

My tourist visa was running out, and Colombia remained a closed door. Still, in my heart, the assurance continued that God, in his time, would make it possible for me to serve him there.

On December 2, I was informed that due to repeated refusals of my application for a Colombian visa, I should go to Quito. In Quito, I could get the necessary papers to travel to the Ecuadorian consul in Ipiales, Colombia. There, I could obtain a permanent visa for Ecuador. You could not receive a visa for the country where you resided. You had to cross into another country. It seemed a little ironic that I would have to cross into the country where I wanted to live to get a visa to a different country because they would not grant me a visa to it.

I traveled all day and night and then until noon the next day over the beautiful Ecuadorian mountains. It was gorgeous but a bit disconcerting at times. In places, it seemed that the train tracks were hanging in midair. As I looked out of the window, the only thing I could see was miles of empty space below. The landscape was breathtaking. Viewing the enormity of God's beautiful creation was an amazing experience.

It took time to get all the paperwork done in Quito. From Quito, I traveled with some missionaries from another mission to Tulcan, Ecuador, which is on the Colombian border. We traveled all day December 9 and arrived about 10:30 p.m. The next morning, I was up early and went to the immigration office on the Ecuadorian side to get instructions about what I must do to cross over into Colombia. With the instructions finally in hand, I returned to the missionary home where I had spent the night. The plan was for one of them to accompany me into Colombia and back.

Just as I arrived, I was called to the ham radio where I received this message: "Return immediately to Guayaquil. Your Colombian visa has been granted!" In 10 minutes, I would have been on my way to cross the border to receive a resident visa for Ecuador. God had granted my Colombian visa just in time. With my traveling suitcase, I started the overland train journey back to Guayaquil that same afternoon. I was going to work in Colombia!

During the next few hours, a whole range of emotions flooded me. Surprisingly, sadness was one of the emotions. I wondered how I was going to tell the dear missionaries and Ecuadorians, with whom I had so lovingly bonded, that I would soon be leaving for Colombia instead of staying in Ecuador.

As I traveled those long hours from Tulcan to Guayaquil, I felt as though Jesus was sitting right beside me—in person. The hours passed quickly as I cried, laughed, and rejoiced. I felt God was saying, "Millie, you have passed the test. Now you may enter the promised land."

I chose to extend my Ecuadorian tourist visa for a few days so I could complete some projects. I had been working with some youth for two months on a Christmas drama they were going to present the Thursday and Sunday before Christmas. This extra time also allowed me to visit the tuberculosis sanatorium, friends in local churches, and each of the groups where I had been teaching children's Bible classes. Saying good-bye was difficult.

I came to the realization that I had needed the time in San Jose and Ecuador to prepare for the work God had for me in Colombia. Leaving my comfort zone and loved ones was a challenge, but my success as a missionary depended on my willingness to trust God in every circumstance. He was training me to be ready to accept his leading in my life. Had he not said, "Trust in the LORD with all thine heart; and lean not unto thine own understanding. In all thy ways acknowledge him, and he will direct thy paths."?

Two days after Christmas, I boarded the 11:00 flight to Quito, where I had a 40-minute layover. My best friend from language school met me there. June Wade and I had an encouraging visit. We prayed for the work that both of us would be doing in our separate mission fields.

I arrived that afternoon in Medellín, Colombia. What a joy! It was God's timing. He had unlocked the door.

*****

Millie's insight: When we are willing to follow God's leading, he empowers us with the abilities needed to accomplish his tasks.

CHAPTER THREE

Planting the Seed
Spreading the Gospel

"All they asked was that we should continue to remember the poor, the very thing I was eager to do." Galatians 2:10

*****

Millie's insight: We may not be the one who has the privilege of seeing a person come to Christ, but we must be faithful to sow the seed.

*****

It didn't take long for me to turn my concern for spreading the Gospel and my desire to retain my Spanish language skills into a ministry outreach for children. I reasoned that the children would be less critical of my language mistakes than the adults. So I started teaching in a Sunday school class at the local OMS-related church. Then I started a junior church program, which was a new program for that church. As if that wasn't enough, I even started a children's choir.

Once I grew more confident of my Spanish language skills and I became more familiar with the Colombian culture and people, I felt a desire to focus some of my ministry efforts on the children in the destitute areas of Medellín. On Saturday and Sunday afternoons, I began visiting the poorest areas of the city. Focusing my attention on the children was the best idea I could have had. First, it placed me in the middle of the Colombian people. I would become well acquainted with their culture. Second, once the children were involved, the parents became interested in the Gospel, and my ministry grew. I was able to evangelize children and adults at the same time.

Of all the places where poor people lived in Medellín, I chose the poorest. In this very impoverished area, the people lived on land that actually belonged to the railroad company. Commercial enterprises were forbidden to locate that close to the railroad track. The little houses were made of cardboard boxes or beaten-out tin cans, and they had dirt floors. Those houses generally only had one room, but sometimes a room divider was used. The living conditions were very crowded. These people were illiterate, so they could not secure jobs that paid enough to raise themselves out of the extreme poverty.

Family planning didn't happen. It was quite common for a family to have 15 or 16 children, but only 4 would still be living. My missionary friends and I used to laugh and say, "Oh, that is an *antioqueño*." By this we meant that person came from the department (state) of Antioquia. This area of Colombia was known for having very large families. Almost all families had at least 12 children.

During the early years, the poor areas of Medellín were dangerous, but they weren't as dangerous as the smaller towns. In the large metropolitan area of Medellín, the radical, violent segment of the state church did not have as much influence as it did in smaller communities. Also during the time I was doing my children's ministry in these extremely poor areas of Medellín, the guerilla activity had not become much of a threat yet.

The mission compound had a little panel truck that I used to drive to the areas of town where I was telling children about the love of Jesus and the salvation he offers. Generally, I went to the area by the railroad tracks on Sunday afternoons. I usually went alone even though I invited others to go with me. Once in a while, someone else would choose to help me. I especially invited seminary students to join me because I believed it was an excellent way for them to hone their teaching and ministry skills.

I was encouraged because my ministry to the very poor was going well. I had discovered a Christian family in the area who invited me to use their little hut to have the meetings for the children. It was a special joy for me to occasionally take some of the missionary kids from the mission school with me. They would help hand out tracts to people who passed by. At the school during the Christmas season, the missionary kids (MKs) would put on a Christmas play in English. Those kids could speak both English and Spanish fluently. So they wore their little costumes and performed the Christmas drama in Spanish for the children who lived by the railroad tracks. It was an excellent way to get the MKs involved in ministry.

The railroad track ministry grew. Many times, all the children and their parents could not fit into the little hut, so we gathered in front of the house. Sometimes 20, 30, or more children were present. The adults often stood around the outer edge of the children and listened.

One Sunday, Emilio, the Christian head of the house where I held my children's meetings, told me about a man who lived down the path a little way. This man was very ill. He had requested that I visit him when I came to the area again, and I agreed to do so. That Sunday, a new, single missionary accompanied me.

Vi Hayes decided to go with me to visit the ill gentleman. We drove down the path as far as we could go in the little green panel truck. When we could go no farther, I parked it and asked one of the older boys from my children's class to watch the truck while we went deeper into the slum to see the man who was so ill. We shared the plan of salvation with him and prayed for him. All seemed to be going well.

On the walk back to where the truck was parked, just as I was able to catch sight of it, I noticed a loud mob of people coming down the path. They were yelling, "We don't want the Protestants! Out with the Protestants!"

As we walked closer to the crowd, one woman stood out from the rest. She was a rather large-built woman, and she was leading the mob. Her eyes were strange and frightening. They were huge and glaring. She put her hand in her ample hair and pulled out on it as she gritted her teeth. She hissed through her teeth, "Down with you!"

For the first time in my life, I was sure I was seeing a demon-possessed woman. We were scared. I was unsure about how to handle the situation. If handled wrong, it could be quite threatening. We might be in peril no matter what we did. None of my training included ideas on how to handle mobs led by a demon-possessed woman.

As I contemplated what to do—find a place to hide, confront the mob, try to find a way around the mob—I saw one of the seminary students coming down the path behind the mob. This young seminary student had not come to the area before, but on that day in that grave situation, he was there. I thought, *Thank you, Lord. Now if I can just get Juan to get up on the front of the truck and begin reading the Bible, perhaps we can quiet the crowd by using God's Word.*

I was able to say to Juan, "Please open your Bible to a passage of Scripture you feel the Lord leading you to for this time. Stand on the front of the truck and read it in a loud voice."

The crowd did quiet some. By the time he finished reading the passage, a few people in the crowd had started to disperse. I turned the truck around, and we inched back toward where we had entered. Juan walked in front of the truck to keep the people out of the way as I drove back. We crept along. I could see some of the more violent crowd members picking up stones to throw at the truck to break the windows. Miraculously, no stones were thrown. As we drove out, I wondered if I should hold the planned meeting at the home of the Christian family or should we just leave the settlement.

I worried about leaving that Christian family. It was not un-common at that time for radicals to burn the homes of believers. I worried about what physical danger the family might face. Would one of them be killed? I got out of the truck, walked up to the house, and told the children a short story. I was more worried about that dear family than for myself, so I spent some time in prayer with the family—praying for God's complete protection for them. We also prayed that the crowd would become calm. The crowd was still outside the house, and a few still had stones in their hands. But the yelling had stopped, and miraculously, some of them were even listening.

We slowly edged the truck out of the area. By the time I reached the main road, the people had dispersed completely and returned to their homes.

At the mission compound, we related what had happened. The first question was, "You won't go back there next week, will you?"

I responded that I had not decided yet. I loved the children and the people to whom I was ministering, and I knew God had led me there to bring his Gospel message to them. I did a lot of praying that week. I sought God's guidance; I desired to do God's will. I recognized that what happened was Satan's way of stopping the Gospel. By not returning, I would allow Satan to have the victory.

Midweek, I told the other missionaries that I would go back to that dangerous area, but I would probably go alone rather than involve too many people.

I safely went back the next Sunday, and I continued to minister in that location until I was asked to take a position at the Peniel Bible Institute located in Cristalina. Because I spent several years in the rural area, I lost contact with the people in that neighborhood.

A few years later, I was visiting in Medellín for several days. During that visit, I attended one of the OMS churches in the city. I was looking forward to visiting that church because I had not seen my Christian friends there for a long time. When I started walking down the aisle that Sunday evening, a lady walked toward me from the front of the church. Just a few feet in front of me, she threw out her arms and said, "Do you remember me?" Her face was familiar to me, but I could not remember who she was.

I replied, "I remember your face, but I do not remember your name."

She said, "I was the woman that was leading the mob when you came into the ghetto area along the railroad track. And I just wanted to let you know that I have been saved and baptized in this church."

I did not hear the story of how she was converted, but it does not matter. I know that sometimes you plant the Gospel and nothing comes of it. You go out there to hoe and plow the Word that has been planted. It may not look like much is happening. I know that many missionaries have spent years planting and watering. God will send timely encouragement to those who are doing his work. That lady's salvation was an encouraging blessing for me. What a pleasure to see how God worked in that area of the city after I left, even though no other missionaries took over my ministry there.

"I planted the seed, Apollos watered it, but God has been making it grow" 1 Corinthians 3:6.

During the first few years I was on the mission field, much of the success that my fellow missionaries and I had in Colombia was in the poor areas of Medellín. I believe this is a fairly universal pattern in Third-World countries. Conversions often begin with the people in lower socioeconomic groups because they have nothing. They cannot say they do not need Jesus. So they bring a different attitude to learning about Jesus. A faith in Jesus gives them something to live for.

*****

Millie's insight: Once you have the children, you have the parents taking part and listening to God's Word.

CHAPTER FOUR

Hiding God's Word
Spreading the Gospel

"How can a young man keep his way pure? By living according to your word. I have hidden your word in my heart that I might not sin against you. Your word is a lamp to my feet and a light for my path." Psalm 119: 9, 11, 105

*****

Millie's insight: The hidden Word in our hearts will light our paths.

*****

In spite of all of the danger we faced, I witnessed the hunger the rural Colombian people had for God's Word. I heard testimonies about the new believers who were compelled to witness and seek opportunities to learn more about God's Word. This seemed to be especially true of the teens and young adults who came to a saving faith. The majority of the work I did in Colombia was with children, teens, and young adults.

I arrived in Colombia in December 1955. During those early years on the mission field, I was stationed in Medellín, teaching missionary children as my primary responsibility and voluntarily working with Colombian children. The mission leadership gave me permission to attend a Youth for Christ convention, which was held in Caracas, Venezuela. During that convention, the Bible Quiz program that Youth for Christ had implemented successfully in the United States was being promoted. I immediately recognized the possibilities for the program in

Colombia. I returned to the mission compound with all the rules and regulations, but they were written in English. I secured help getting them translated into Spanish, as I still was not fluent enough to complete the task on my own. Once I felt the call of God, I enthusiastically and tenaciously proceeded to follow his command.

I first started the Bible Quiz program in Medellín with the teens in the OMS-related church there. The only other OMS-related church close enough to include in the Bible Quiz was in Puerto Berrio. I took the Medellín team to Puerto Berrio to show that church how it was done so they could start a team there. The four teens and I embarked on the eight-hour train trip. We traveled on Friday and were to make the return trip on Monday. Howard Biddulph, a missionary kid, was among the youth traveling with me. He was a freshman that year. He became an enthusiastic Bible Quiz team member for the rest of his high school years.

The first year, I challenged the youth to memorize the book of John. The rural youth embraced the challenge of memorizing a whole book of the Bible. The students became more excited as their first competition approached because they had been working very hard on the memorization and were proud of their progress thus far.

Once I saw how the Colombian youth were embracing the Bible Quiz challenge, I went to Bogotá to present the program. From there I traveled to Barbosa to promote Bible Quiz. Now I had four teams, and I worked with them every chance I could get.

The mission leadership wanted to have a special event for the teenage Christians in the OMS churches. With hopes of making it an annual event, we planned a youth congress at the Bible Institute in Cristalina. I was excited about the possibility of getting the four teams together for a competition. The leadership approved a competition as a preliminary event before the main activities. Unfortunately, the team from Barbosa was unable to attend because they could not raise enough funds, which was disappointing as they had memorized and studied the book of John diligently.

The three teams that did attend had either completely memorized the book of John or were very close to it. I do have to admit those young people memorized more of John than I had, but I probably knew about all of it by the time we had the competition. I had made out all the questions and worked with the youth. My knowledge of John's Gospel was fairly extensive by the end of that year.

On Friday night before the first quiz, the teens from all three teams and their leaders met together. It was precious to watch the young people practice and drill each other on their knowledge of the passages and their memorization of verses. Even though they were in a competition and wanted to win first place, the spirit of the competitors was wonderful. Yes, they wanted to win, but it was not a cutthroat competition. They became acquainted quickly despite marked differences in the economic backgrounds of some of the team members. It did not matter if they were from a very poor rural area or from a more privileged family living in Bogotá. They bonded with each other and encouraged each other, no matter what team they represented. Each teen recognized the determination and dedication the other youth had for memorizing Scripture.

At that first Colombian youth conference of the OMS-related churches, the activities were kicked off with the Bible Quiz contest. I had mission institute workers help with score keeping and judging which contestant was the first to jump to his or her feet to answer the question. The contestants received final instructions on how the competition would be conducted and where they were to stand. The excitement in the air was palpable.

The intelligence and talent of the youth for memorizing Scripture was remarkable. They did not have a lot of unimportant stuff filling their minds. Some of the kids on those rural teams had not even had a chance to complete a fifth-grade level education. They filled their heads and hearts with the Gospel. The kids from the river area held their own in the competition, and the more privileged teens from Bogotá recognized and respected their abilities.

During that first conference, OMS accepted the Bible Quiz program as an official part of the youth congress for the next year. We set a goal to have representatives from every region where OMS had established churches. We planned to have regional encounters to form a team from the winners of those competitions. We would then bring the regional teams to the youth congress for a final championship competition. I did a lot of traveling during my summer vacation that year. I drummed up enthusiasm and encouraged older members of youth groups or other interested individuals to spearhead the local study and competitions. Almost every OMS-related church had a competition. The next year OMS sponsored 13 regional conferences and brought those teams to the youth congress at Cristalina.

This program was a lively part of my teen ministry for several years. Each year we focused on a different book of the Bible. Many of the original participants memorized as many as five or six books before they graduated out of the program. The impact of this program was amazing. Unfortunately it eventually started to decline, but no matter. For several years over a large area of rural Colombia, it encouraged the memorization of the Scriptures in such a way that only a spirited friendly competition can accomplish.

I remember reporting back to the Bible Quiz organization in the United States. I was so enthusiastic about the success of the program with the people of Colombia. I remember ending the letter by saying, "Praise the Lord. It can be done in Colombia too."

Sometimes, years after I had ceased working with the Bible Quiz teams, I would be thrilled to hear from some of the Bible Quiz kids about how learning those Scriptures and the relationships developed during the study and competitions had influenced their lives. About the time I retired from full-time mission work, Howard Biddulph, while conversing with me, told me how important my ministry had been to him.

Howard said, "Aunt Millie, did you know that you are the one who had a major influence on my coming back as a full-time missionary to Colombia?"

I was a little surprised by the statement, and it must have shown on my face because he continued by saying, "One of the things that influenced me most was those Bible quizzes. We got so much out of that, and we learned so much of the Scripture. The other thing was that I saw how you could go to those places and continue on for years. I thought that if someone as little as you can do that, surely I could do something on the mission field."

When I was attending the 100th anniversary celebration for OMS in 2001, I had a conversation with one of the Colombian pastors who attended. He said, "Doña Mildred, do you know where I got my start of really feeling God's call on my life? It was studying for those Bible quizzes."

You never know how intently studying and learning God's word, memorizing verses, and asking each other questions about the Scriptures can impact lives. Those youth worked hard. Little groups of teens could be seen studying and praying into the early morning hours. The young people were committed to learning the Word, not just a surface understanding, but at a deeper level.

*****

Millie's insight: When people have the desire to live a pure life according to God's Word, it is easy to hide it in their hearts.

CHAPTER FIVE

Do Not Move Another Inch
Obeying God's Command

"But God said to Balaam, 'Do not go with them...'"
Numbers 22:12a

*****

Millie's insight: God relates to us so often by just a small voice, not necessarily an audible voice. But something within us assures us that God is speaking. At times, God says go; at times, God says wait, it's not the time; and at times, God says stop and go no further.

*****

It was during one of my trips to visit a small mission church in the mountainous regions of Colombia when I experienced God plainly telling me to stop.

I was off to visit a mountain village where OMS had a functioning church, but the Christian day school had been closed. I have such a heart for children that I wanted to witness the situation for myself. I wanted to talk with local believers—to learn from them how I could help facilitate reopening the school.

My heart went out to the people in the small villages that are scattered throughout Colombia. Much of the work I did was in preparing Colombian nationals from these rural areas to become teachers for Christian day schools that were established in villages of 500 to 1,000 people. I trained nationals, and I was able to assist them in starting Christian day schools not only along the rivers and in the jungle areas but also in the mountainous regions. The southern mountainous regions of Colombia were especially dangerous at that time because of the guerillas they called *chusma*. The *chusma* were fighting against the Colombian government and were especially brutal toward people who practiced a different religion than the state religion. They were led by an extreme political and religious zealot finger of the Catholic Church. They were just not happy people.

When the guerilla attacks happened, sometimes a whole family would be killed. Sometimes part of a family would be executed. Always, the family members were forced to give the guerillas their land and any possessions the guerillas desired. As a result, displaced rural families would pour into villages or even into large metropolitan areas such as Bogotá. These rural people had no idea how to live in the populous city, and survival was very difficult for them. Those refugees that made it to close-by villages were somewhat safe, but they faced many problems too. Often one parent had been killed, or sometimes children would arrive in the village with neither parent surviving the guerilla attack on their home.

I knew something about the background of the woman I planned to visit in the small village of Barbosa. Celina Soto was a Christian leader in the village that was inhabited mostly by a fairly radical segment of the state church. A Christian day school had operated in this village before I started traveling to rural areas. But it had been closed for some time because of local vicious attitudes and behaviors against the government and those who were not involved in the Catholic faith as practiced by the extremists in the region. Barbosa was in an area where there was much senseless violence. I wanted to meet with Celina to discern if there was any possibility of reopening the school and to encourage her in the work she was doing for the small mission church.

Members of Celina's family had been in contact with the OMS missionaries for some time. Celina, one of the girls in the Soto family of 12 children, had fled into the mountains to escape the *chusma* attackers. Her parents and young siblings had been forced to flee from their home and hide. Eventually Celina was able to reconnect with society. She settled in Barbosa, which had a church started by OMS.

I knew that traveling to the remote areas was always an adventure. When the mission leadership asked me to visit Celina in Barbosa, I had only a general idea where it was located. The mission leaders gave me directions, and prayers for safe travel were said. Never one to worry about travel details, I set out on the trip. I was confident I was on God's mission, and he would guide. I knew that previously some of the missionaries had almost been killed while working in the region around Barbosa, but the mission leadership would not have sent me if they felt it was too dangerous at that time.

First, I had to fly from Medellín to Bogotá in a two-prop plane. In Bogotá, I purchased a ticket for Barbosa and boarded a train. The trip took hours because it stopped at every town along the way. When it finally arrived at the town of Barbosa, many little boys jumped immediately onto the train calling, "*Maleta* (suitcase). *Maleta. Maleta.*" I looked around and selected two of the boys to carry my suitcases for me. I asked them if they knew where the *casa evangelica* (the evangelical church) was. They answered in the affirmative. After walking several blocks with those young boys, I suddenly experienced a compelling thought. *Don't go with them.* I commanded the boys to stop and asked them, "Do you really know where the *casa evangelica* is?" They replied, "No, but we know where the priest's house is." At that time, in that location, two innocent boys were leading me to possible imprisonment or death.

I told those boys I was not going any farther. They were to leave the suitcases right there. Just at that moment, a young boy walked up to me. He said, "*Señorita*, are you looking for Celina Soto? I know where she lives. I will take you there." He had overheard my conversation with the two boys. I was unaware that anyone was around, but God placed that boy at the right location at the right time to protect me in this dangerous town.

The boy took me to an apartment in the back of the church where Celina lived. She was expecting me, but she did not know the exact day I would arrive. Celina enthusiastically greeted me at the back door. She was thrilled to have a visitor from OMS. Even though we had not met before, I knew we would have a wonderful time discussing God's Word and talking about God's work in Barbosa.

The Sunday church service was held in the afternoon, around 5:00 p.m., because many of the church members had quite a distance to travel. Actually, Sunday in most of Colombia is the market day for the area farmers. They bring produce into town early in the morning to sell to villagers. Church services are held at a time so as not to interfere with the produce market.

Therefore, Celina and I had some time to visit and get to know one another. It was during the morning conversations that I learned the reason I had not been led through the front of the church. A huge padlock firmly locked the front door. But that wasn't all; the town's mayor had put a seal over the padlock. The front doors were locked and sealed shut. The mayor had declared that no one was to go into the church for worship. That sealed padlock had been on the front door of the church for months. However, that did not stop the evangelical worshipers. They just went in the back way. This meant they went through Celina's apartment to enter the church to worship God.

As Celina was showing the town to me, I soon learned that she was one of those Colombian treasures. She had a motherly appearance and a kindly spirit, mixed with an iron will to do as God bids. Her intense passion for the souls of friends and neighbors spilled out from her as she went about the daily activities of village life. Even though she lived in an area that was dangerous for Christians, Celina was determined to stick it out. She was going to serve God, no matter what personal challenges she faced. Sharing the love of her Savior was her passion.

In the middle of giving me a village tour that Sunday morning, Celina looked me in the eye and said she felt she was to break the seal on the lock on the front door of the church. She believed God was leading her to open the doors and welcome the worshipers. To many people, opening the front doors of the church may sound like a sensible step of faith. But it was not, if you are talking about normal good sense in an antagonistic atmosphere. I knew this would be a huge, dangerous risk for her. Celina could easily be arrested and sent to prison, or worse. Nevertheless, she broke the seal at 4:00 p.m. and opened the front doors of the church.

As the service started, I was calm but aware that the situation could rapidly become dangerous. About halfway through the service, a large group of people marched in front of the church, screaming, "Down with the Protestants." The service continued, and worshipers paid little attention to the commotion outside the church doors. Not one believer turned around to see what was happening or even acted slightly concerned. They were there to worship God, and that is what they did. At the end of the service, they had a short, but intense prayer meeting, specifically asking God for protection as they left the church and traveled home.

God answered those prayers. Celina and I went to bed that evening with no fear for our safety.

Refrigerators were very rare in the rural areas of Colombia, so small grocery stores were found in the neighborhoods. People generally bought their food daily. Next to the church was a home that had one room in which the family operated one of these neighborhood grocery stores. Because it was so convenient, Celina did most of her shopping there. She had a good relationship with that family. However, the day after the church's front door was opened, that family would not sell her anything. Celina gently reminded the man that she had purchased her groceries from him for years, and she had never failed to pay him. She asked her neighbor why he would not sell her some oatmeal and milk. His reply was that he was prohibited from selling to her. Celina thanked him and left. She was able to purchase her breakfast items at another location.

I needed some toothpaste. Since the neighborhood grocer did not know me, Celina thought I should be able to purchase toothpaste there. I entered the shop and asked for some Colgate toothpaste. The shopkeeper told me that he had none. But I could see it on the shelf, so I pointed to what I wanted. His responded, "No, I cannot sell it to you."

I reported to Celina that I couldn't buy anything from him either. It was a very long time before that small grocer would sell items to Celina. At that point, whoever had threatened him must have eventually lost influence or the person in power must have loosened their opposition to Celina's little mission church.

God was good to his servant Celina. The punishment for breaking the seal on the padlock and the opening of the front doors to the church could have been much more severe than not being able to buy groceries next door. The people in the community knew services were being held in that little church. They could see people entering through the door of the apartment. They heard the *a cappella* singing of the congregation. All of that was tolerated. But the opening of the doors was more than some of the radical element in that town could tolerate. I must admit that the locals may have been blaming me for the doors being opened because I would have been readily recognized as a foreigner. Praise God, the demonstrators only screamed slogans against us that evening.

Amazingly, that church has never been closed again. Apparently, God used that incident to change the hearts of the local leaders. Maybe it was because of God's work through Celina and other local believers. It makes no difference how God chose to work the miracle of faith, but he did. Eventually they were also able to reopen the Christian day school.

After that experience, I took special pleasure in traveling to visit my friend, the spiritual giant, Celina. But let it be known, I never asked how to get to the church again. The road to the little mission church God had established in Barbosa was imprinted on my mind.

*****

Millie's insight: When the Holy Spirit is leading us, he sometimes leads in ways that are beyond our wildest imaginations.

CHAPTER SIX

Broken and Spilled Out

"While Jesus was in Bethany in the home of a man known as Simon the Leper, a woman came to him with an alabaster jar of very expensive perfume, which she poured on his head as he was reclining at the table. When the disciples saw this, they were indignant. 'Why this waste?' they asked. 'This perfume could have been sold at a high price and the money given to the poor.' Aware of this, Jesus said to them, 'Why are you bothering this woman? She has done a beautiful thing to me.'"
Matthew 26:6–10

*****

Millie's insight: Many people who are broken and spilled out will never have their names recorded in history. Many of humble origin will pour out their lives for Jesus Christ, and we will never know it.

*****

Lester Erny is one of those people that most would pass by, thinking he was a burden on society because of his physical appearance and abilities. But he was an amazing servant of Jesus Christ, effectively spreading the light to many people.

Lester had a horrible mishap right after he celebrated his 18th birthday. A swimming accident left him paralyzed. In seconds, he went from being a vibrant young man to being unable to move his arms or legs.

I only vaguely knew Lester before his accident. I first met him at Wichita North High School. He also occasionally attended Wesley United Methodist Church in north Wichita, Kansas, where I attended. Lester and I had no more chance contacts for several years as I was in college while Lester was healing and learning to live with severe disabilities.

A few days after I arrived home in 1959 on my first home ministry assignment (HMA), I received a phone call. It only took me a moment to realize to whom I was talking. It was Lester, my distant friend from high school who had miraculously survived a swimming accident—the accident 10 years earlier that left him bedfast for the remainder of his life. I was quite surprised to receive this call from him. Lester requested that I visit him. As an encouragement to me, he sang a lovely hymn. I could not believe the voice I heard. It was beautiful. Just beautiful.

I gathered up my slides and projector and traveled to Lester's home in north Wichita. I wanted to show him some of the ministry I was doing in Colombia. He was interested in my work and asked many questions, not only about the mission but also about Colombia. And we had a peaceful time of prayer together.

During that visit, Lester gave his testimony. He said that in the quietness placed upon him after his accident, he had found Christ as his Savior. Since that time, he witnessed to others about the love of Jesus every chance he had. He had been breaking and pouring out perfume on scores and scores of people.

Lester found ways to express himself and to share his love for Jesus. He had learned to move his elbow around a certain way so he could manipulate some things, and he had learned to paint by putting the brush in his mouth. By using a stylus, he could dial the telephone. One of his ministries was to call an individual when he learned that person was discouraged. He would call hurting people, talk with them, and pray with them.

Lester had a small income from the Social Security disability program. This money provided some assistance in paying for his care. Lester could not be in the house by himself, so someone was always with him. When I visited him the first time, he was living with his mother. His father had already passed away.

The people at the Evangelical Methodist Church, in north Wichita, had a van modified so they could slip Lester off his bed onto a special bed that fit in the van. They would transport him to various area churches where he would sing. He sang of his love for Jesus and inspired many through this ministry.

Toward the end of that first visit, after we had prayed, I loaded my projector and slides into the car. Then I walked back into the house to say goodbye to Lester and his mother. Lester asked me to come closer to his bed. With the right elbow of his shriveled arm, he pushed a wrinkled $2 bill to the side of the bed. Lester said, "I want this to go to your mission work."

My eyes immediately welled up in tears. I thought, *Here is this young man in this tragic condition, yet he is giving his first gift to missions. What a sacrificial gift!* Shortly after that, he took out a $5 a month share in my support. When the cost of the support shares for OMS was increased, Lester increased his support. He kept his faith promise until his dying day in 2008.

Lester will never appear in a list of giants of faith compiled by men, but he is on God's list of faith heroes.

The work of the missionary does not only happen overseas but back home as well. The support and prayers of many people make the work of missionaries possible. The sacrifices of missionaries make the growth of the body of evangelic Christians possible in amazing ways in other countries. Believers' prayers and sacrifices are a pleasing aroma, a perfume poured out for God that permeates the world.

As a result of the work of OMS missionaries, I believe a person who will appear on God's list of faith heroes is a Colombian lady named Nery Ramírez. I remember the day a plane arrived in Medellín with Nery and her two little girls accompanying the body of her husband, who had been the pastor of the OMS church in the village of Zaragosa, down on the river. Just 10 days before Christmas, he had climbed on the front of that little church to put up a lighted cross. It was to symbolize Christ as the light of the world. One of the bricks he was grasping gave way, and he fell. He died a few hours later in the hospital.

When Nery arrived in Medellín, her family, local mission-aries, and believers from the OMS church met her. Nery's first words were to her older sister, "Ovelia, will you go back with me to help finish the preparations for the Christmas program that we are to present on Christmas Eve?" It was almost unbelievable how little concern she had for herself and how much concern she had for the ministry to the Zaragosa community through that little church.

Nery returned to minister to her community through the Christmas services. She and her husband had poured out all they had as they ministered to their little congregation of believers in that remote river community.

Nery stayed in the ministry. She attended the Bible institute to better prepare herself for the ministry she had. She took those two little girls with her even when God called her into some very rough locations. Nery continued to be poured-out per-fume, permeating the people around her. I have remained in contact with Nery over the years. When I returned to the U.S., I continued contact through emails with the girls and occasional letters to Nery.

On December 18, 1976, I was living on the third floor of an apartment building on the bank of the Magdalena River. It had been 10 months since my husband's death, and I was moving to Medellín to continue my work from there. The flat concrete roof was directly above my apartment. I was alone at that time with my 2½-year-old toddler. My two daughters had already traveled to Medellín with Doña Nery's teenage daughter, Esther. It was a blessing to know my daughters were being cared for and protected as I was completing the last-minute packing of my household. The filling of the 55-gallon steel drums was almost complete. I was packing suitcases and super-vising the delivery of furniture to anybody who would take it.

At 4:00 that last morning, I climbed the stairs to be alone with the Lord. I looked out over the Magdalena River. It was like a never-ending ribbon, running in both directions. The morning was gorgeous. Two years earlier, Vernon and I had stood together on that roof. We held hands and said to each other, "This is the place God has given us to work, and we want to pour out our lives for these river people." As I stood on the roof this day, Vernon had already poured out his lifeblood for Jesus, the one he so dearly loved. I stood there as a young widow. That morning, I felt as though I was breaking a bottle of perfume and pouring it out over that river. I was asking the Lord to use me to reach the hundreds of lives throughout the river area.

*****

Millie's insight: One who is broken for Jesus Christ can make a difference that may never be recognized in the halls of fame, but they will shed light in the dark world for others. Jesus recognizes the beautiful things people do to bring light to this world—anointing with perfume, poured out in love. It is important to remember the humble servants not only in Colombia but also in the United States who have been an important part of my mission. Are you ready to pour out your life—to break the bottle of perfume and pour it out for Jesus?

CHAPTER SEVEN

Making a Change

"You shall see greater things than that." John 1:50b

*****

Millie's insight: God prepares the way for us. Our duty is to obey his leading, and God will show us greater things.

*****

We can often, quite easily, become comfortable with our current situation. Few surprises interrupt our activities. We know what to expect. Life is predictable. But then suddenly, God directs us to break out of our comfort zone because he has finished training us in that situation. God wants us to serve him in faith, knowing he is in total control—knowing he has prepared the way.

I loved teaching and had a true love for the Colombian people, so after 6½ years of working with missionary children, I was asked to change my focus from teaching at the mission compound to working with Colombians in the United Christian School in Medellín. The Presbyterian mission group ran it for the Colombian children who had Christian parents. They needed someone to serve as an administrator while their principal went on HMA to the United States. I was selected because I understood education, had been a successful teacher, had a heart for children, and related well with the Colombian people. I was glad

43

to work the final six months of the school year in that position, but I longed for the day the principal would return. The Lord was creating a desire in my heart to train Colombians to teach children in the rural areas. It seemed like an impossible dream, but God was preparing the way.

A few years earlier, the rural Colombian Christian young people had requested that the missionaries provide some Bible training beyond what they received from itinerant missionaries. These young Christians felt the call to act as pastors in their communities but knew they needed theological training. So the Peniel Bible Institute was launched in 1955 with a short session held on the grounds of the Colombian Bible Seminary in Medellín because there was no other viable location available. However, the OMS missionaries soon started looking for land in the rural areas. We felt it was important to move the Bible institute out of the city because we wanted graduates to go into the rural areas to minister to those who had limited exposure to Gospel truth. The consensus was that we could reach more people in the rural areas if our training facility was in a central location away from the metropolitan areas.

Land was purchased just outside of Cristalina, a small rural town. Even with the change of location, many obstacles had to be overcome if the Colombians were going to become the source of instruction in the Christian day schools. How were we to find youth willing to become rural teachers? How were we to ensure that those youth had a vibrant faith and a sufficient level of biblical knowledge? Who would do the training, and how would it be funded? After being trained, would the youth be willing to go into the rural areas where schools were so desperately needed? Those who were brought into the city for training often did not desire to return to the subsistence level of living found in the rural areas. How were we going to train Colombians and, at the same time, encourage them to return to the impoverished rural areas that were in such desperate need of reading skills and had not heard about the love of God for them?

Some Colombian Christians had gone out to start schools, but they had no real training and were only moderately successful. I recognized the desperate need for training primary teachers. Because of my experiences ministering to children in the slums of Medellín, I understood the best way to win the adults to Christ was through God working in the hearts of their children. God placed a burden on my heart to train Christian teachers at the Cristalina campus. Because of my God-given gifts and my love for the Colombian people, the mission leadership recognized that I was uniquely prepared by God to start the Christian teacher-training department. Since I knew God had called, I moved out of my comfort zone in Medellín into a new ministry in rural Colombia.

Teaching materials were limited, but I learned to be very resourceful with flannel graph pictures and other simple supplies. Most of the students, even though they were teenagers, had no experience with scissors or other basic items found in all North American schools.

I became the local mimeograph machine expert. All the other instructors at the Bible institute would bring their stencils to me so I could produce the needed copies on that machine. Apparently, I had a special talent that was a blessing to the other instructors. Later, my husband said that he found me while I was running that old mimeograph machine. Vernon told how he came up to the window and saw this young lady with ink almost up to her elbows and on her face. He thought, *Poor girl.*

I should have been a bit dismayed as an eligible male came into my life while I was inking that messy machine. However, I was too busy to take much notice at that time. After we were married, Vernon told me his first thoughts about me. I replied, "So you married me for pity."

I often made jokes about that challenging machine, but actually I felt blessed to have a way to produce teaching materials in that rural location and to help the others. God had given me a servant's heart. How else could my willingness to make copies for everyone else in addition to copying my materials be explained?

A train station with a small store was the only place close by to purchase needed items, so most supplies had to be ordered from outside and shipped to our rural location. Even our mail had to be sent in on the train from Medellín as there was no local post office. It took eight hours for it to travel to Medellín even though it was only 100 miles away. Since the train was the only link that rural areas had to metropolitan services, it stopped at every small village or station along the way. It was the only somewhat reliable source of transportation and supplies.

Because the small local store could not supply all our needs, the compound had to be fairly self-sufficient. Therefore, we set up a farming operation on the parcel of ground the Bible institute owned. The men cut away some of the jungle to make room for the campus and to make an area available for the farming operation. Cattle, chickens, and horses were all raised and cared for there. Some of the animals raised on the institute farm would be butchered to provide part of the needed meat. However, the small farming operation could not supply enough meat to meet the needs of a campus with more than 100 individuals to feed. Thankfully, the people who ran the store at the train station were able to supply most of our meat. A vegetable garden was always planted and tended, which helped too. We gathered eggs from the chickens we raised, and once or twice a week, egg crates full of eggs would be sent to Medellín with a list of needed supplies and the outgoing mail. The Medellín missionaries would sell or use the eggs, buy the items on the shopping list, pack the crates, and place incoming mail in the egg crates

The staff at Peniel Bible Institute had to plan well. When visitors came, they ate what we had. There wasn't anywhere to go to find anything else. One time, when a group of youth and their sponsors were scheduled to visit the Bible institute, a flood where they were to board the train prevented their timely departure. So they did not arrive until a day late. Unfortunately, word could not be sent to me. I had prepared a meal for 20 people that had to be stored until the next day. We did have refrigerators and a couple of freezers that were used by the campus and staff. So I cooled the food and refrigerated it.

The next day, I heated the baked potatoes and was taking them out of the oven when the pan I was using buckled. All the hot baked potatoes hit the concrete floor. What was I to do? I had no way to replace the potatoes, and washing them in water would cool them down. So I brushed them off, put them on the table, and gave instructions. I told my guests that they were not to eat the skins. They were to scoop the insides of the potatoes out and place the skins in a dish I had provided for that purpose. Knowing they had to make some adjustments to their normal dietary practices so they would not become ill, they all followed my directions without any questions. No one became sick, and no one knew what had happened back in the kitchen until several months later when I decided to confess.

Due to our remote location, everyone had to live on campus—teachers, support staff, and students. But don't get the idea that Peniel Bible Institute was a one-room schoolhouse-sized operation. The student enrollment varied between 90 and 120 students. The staff included instructors, farm administrators, dorm parents, office workers, and kitchen workers. Approximately 15 staff members and their families lived on campus.

Because we did not have the physical facilities to house both boys and girls during the first two years after the Bible institute moved to the rural location, only boys were enrolled. Some had only three years of education. The most remote areas had little, if any, access to even primary schools. In many of the rural areas, the children of evangelical parents were not allowed in the public schools. If they were allowed to attend public schools, they were persecuted. Sometimes, they were made to kneel in the hot sun for a long period of time, they were verbally abused, they may have had stones thrown at them, and they suffered other forms of cruelty. No one can blame them for refusing to attend those abusive schools.

In just a few years, the institute developed into a four-year training program for pastors and teachers. The facility was operated by OMS, but Christians from denominations other than OMS attended the Bible institute. Occasionally, students from larger metropolitan areas like Bogotá and Medellín would attend classes. But the majority of the students were from small rural villages.

Students attending the Peniel Bible Institute would study half a day and provide labor on the farm the other half-day. The staff divided the students into four groups. While two groups were working, the other two were studying.

OMS developed a scholarship plan to help the students pay for their studies. The funding was raised as the missionaries presented the need to churches and Christian groups when they were in the United States on HMA.

It didn't take me long to realize that I needed a way to give my prospective teachers some classroom practice. So I started a little school in the back of the chapel. Some of the students had children. Those children and the children of Colombian faculty members attended. Children from the small village were invited, but few accepted that offer. When I was not teaching my classes, I would observe the student teachers as they did their practice teaching.

Later we moved the children's school to a building in the village that was used by the institute for church services. When we moved the small school into the village, more of the village children attended. The parents were able to see the fine education the children were receiving from the student teachers who were working under my supervision.

Men for Missions, a ministry of OMS, was helpful to us. Men for Missions teams regularly traveled to Colombia to help us with building projects and in other areas as needed. One of those teams built a primary school on the campus. That was a wonderful solution to the problem of having a suitable location for teachers to practice teaching children.

Several years later, when I returned from HMA in the United States, our oldest daughter Colleen was a beneficiary of the excellent education those young beginning teachers provided. Colleen had finished all the requirements for kindergarten while living in the United States. So rather than have her sit out the rest of the semester when we returned to Colombia, I put her in first grade at the little campus school for the Colombian children. Colleen learned to read in Spanish before she learned how to read in English. It was with delight and pride that I watched my student teachers teaching my own daughter to read Spanish.

*****

Millie's insight: One of the most powerful ministries in Christian work is preparing the local workers to take over ministries in their own language and culture. Training hundreds of Colombian youth for evangelizing and teaching multiplied our outreach.

CHAPTER EIGHT

Hidden Treasure

"I will give you the treasures of darkness, riches stored in secret places, so that you may know that I am the LORD, the God of Israel, who summons you by name." Isaiah 45:3

*****

Millie's insight: The most precious jewels in Colombia are not its emeralds, but its lovely people.

*****

Many people do not realize that Colombia is a country of hidden treasures. The majority of the world's emeralds are found there. Coal mines are productive. The country has spectacular landscapes, as three ranges of the Andes Mountains are located there. Its landscape is green all year because of its proximity to the equator.

Areas away from large cities are challenging to reach because of rough, mountainous terrain and frequent severe flooding in low-lying areas. For this reason many people live in regions where they receive little or no exposure to what citizens of the United States would consider basic necessities. Nevertheless, the Colombian people are its greatest resource.

When I first established a residence in Medellín, my purpose was to take the Gospel to the Colombian people, although my official job was to teach the children of missionaries in the mission compound. It was advantageous for the missionaries of various denominations and from different mission organizations in the same geographic area to work together toward educating their English-speaking children.

My double majors in education and Bible were excellent preparation for this assignment. I served as a teacher for the children of missionaries for 6½ years on the Medellín compound. Generally, 20 to 25 missionary kids (MKs) attended the OMS school where I taught. I considered it a joy to work with those children. The parents were supportive and backed me in every way. But most important to me was the opportunity to encourage those MKs to follow Christ always.

On the mission field, most Christian denominations tend to work together. We regularly combined our efforts on evangelistic campaigns, Christmas activities, Easter worship services, and celebrations of various kinds. The daily challenges that the small groups of missionaries faced drew us together in support of each other. For as Jesus said in Mark 3:25, "If a house is divided against itself, that house cannot stand." These words are never truer than on the mission field. The missionaries in Colombian functioned as a true Christian family.

At the time I arrived, making headway in the state of Antioquia was difficult. Christians were killed for their faith. Others were beaten or tortured and left for dead. Missionaries often were able to get appropriate medical help for some of these individuals. The persecution in the Medellín area was so intense that God's work was being thwarted. OMS knew that the Lord was leading us to extend our evangelistic work to the people living in small villages along the rivers and in the rural areas.

In the 1940s, the missionaries creatively came up with a new approach to reach people living in rural areas along the rivers and streams. OMS built a river launch on which the missionaries could eat, sleep, and travel. Missionaries and Colombian converts evangelized small villages as they traveled up and down the rivers. In an effort to cover as much territory as possible, they would stop at a river village for two days and hold meetings then move on to the next little settlement. The truth about God was getting out, but the river people were hungry for more. Christian youth begged the missionaries to give them further training.

The work done from this little launch on the rivers was amazing. Zeal to spread the Gospel developed in the hearts of many of the new converts. These young Christians spread the Gospel even though their physical safety was doubtful. Often, they quietly held a service in someone's home, but they didn't dare sing. If someone walking by the hut heard them singing Christian songs, those dear Christians would find their home burned. The burning of the homes of believers happened frequently in the 1940s through the mid-1950s.

In some villages during periods of unrest, it was too dangerous to be seen in public with a Bible because of persecution from extremist groups operating there. Believers still attended services held in homes, but they carried their Bibles wrapped in a newspaper or camouflaged in some manner. If a Bible were seen, it would be confiscated and destroyed.

Before the mid-1960s, Bibles could not be taken into Colombia for distribution. Missionaries and Colombians were forbidden to have shipments of Bibles delivered. However, a foreigner could take a single personal Bible into the country. So a Bible was a precious possession and lovingly protected. The state church, until the late 1960s when Pope Paul VI visited Colombia, forbade laity to read the Bible. A contingent of the Catholic Church membership was disturbed by the fact that Bible reading was forbidden. Some even defiantly attended Bible studies in the homes of Christian friends because of their desire to learn more about Jesus Christ.

In a meeting during the pope's visit to Bogotá, some brave souls stood in the gathering and addressed him. They asked the pope for an explanation of why only the priests were allowed to read the Bible. They stated that since it was God's Word, they wanted to be permitted to read it. They argued that they did not understand why the Protestants could have the Bible but people who were members of the Catholic church could not.

They created enough of an uproar that the pope saw the need. He ruled that laity could read the Bible.

The evangelicals jumped on that announcement. The evangelic missionary groups notified their organizations, and the American Bible Society in the United States sent shipments of Bibles. We took Bibles into the rural settlements and distributed them in the cities.

As a result of the pope's ruling, evangelical Christians were invited into the Catholic schools to tell Bible stories. Teachers in the Catholic schools had little knowledge of Bible stories because they had no opportunity to read the Bible until that time.

Vernon and I busied ourselves making marionettes to use for teaching children the Bible. A school located close to the mission compound in Medellín invited us to conduct a marionette performance at an assembly for their students. We presented a Bible story and a fairy tale. After our initial performance, the principal asked us to come back but to bring only Bible stories the next time. The pope's decision definitely gave missionaries an opening to teach the Bible and to distribute Bibles to the Colombian people.

Wherever a state church exists in a country, persons who do not practice that faith can be in great danger because of the control the church officials have over the people. In Colombia, the state church is the Catholic Church, and it exerts much pressure on the people to conform to its desires. During some of my time I on the mission field, the church organization was a dogmatic organization, and in some areas of the country, it was intolerant and cruel. They influenced or ran everything—including the government and the schools. Religious freedom was nonexistent.

The first Christian day schools were started in the cities in the mid-1950s. They were intended for children of Christian parents or for families who were sympathetic to the Gospel. In many areas, the children of evangelical Christians were either not allowed to attend school or were persecuted. Harrowing tales about the treatment of these children were common. In one instance, a teacher told the children to throw rocks at a Christian classmate during recess. The persecuted children often quit attending school because of the discriminatory or cruel treatment.

At various times over the years, the government closed the Christian schools we had started in the rural areas because they were not accredited. Getting accreditation was impossible because they were not Catholic. The government called the missionaries Protestants and accused us of proselytizing. When the government closed the schools, it caused frustration and discouragement, but in faith and with God's direction, we persevered. Eventually, we were able to open some schools again.

I had been on the mission field only a few years when a site close to the small village of Cristalina was selected as the permanent home for the newly established Peniel Bible Institute, which was founded to train rural pastors and teachers. From the compound on clear days, one could see the Magdalena River, Colombia's largest river. This location had few amenities, but it was accessible to the rural Christians. All necessities had to be shipped in by train from Medellín or Puerto Berrio.

Because I knew how badly the children in rural areas needed well-trained teachers, I set about developing a four-year teacher-training program. I wanted my students at the end of the four years to be academically and spiritually prepared to return to the rural areas as Christian teachers.

The missionary community encouraged me as I developed the new teacher-training program. However, no acceptable pedagogy books in Spanish were available, so I used the books I had studied in my teacher-training program at Friends University in Wichita, Kansas, as resources. Apparently God's prompting was the reason I had taken my teacher preparation books to Colombia. The Bible institute was able to obtain Spanish language ministerial textbooks from other countries; however, the materials I needed for teacher training were unavailable to me from outside sources. I used the most relevant and essential parts from my pedagogy books for the teacher-training program. I readily admit that my translation skills at that time were not well-honed, but I had to have materials to use with my students. Besides giving instruction on how to teach basic reading, writing, and arithmetic, I also taught Bible and grammar. The students only had four years at the Bible institute to fine-tune their reading and math skills, to learn what was in the curriculum, to develop teaching skills, and to enhance their Bible knowledge.

I became acquainted with the public school curriculum to ensure that all the necessary components were included in the training of those prospective teachers. I was free to incorporate religious instruction into my training because it was a part of the official government school's curriculum. The study of the Bible was identified as religion, not as evangelical instruction. As long as the Bible instruction was specified as religion, it was allowed.

The Christian day schools were very careful to never make the distinction that only evangelicals could attend their schools, for that would have limited their influence. The schools were there to expose the unsaved to the Gospel of Jesus Christ. The teachers were honest with prospective students and their parents. All new students were told that religion would be based on the Bible and taught from the Bible. They assured the parents that the children would not be forced to pray but Christian morals, standards, and beliefs would be taught. In the beginning, parents were required to sign a document, stating they understood these facts.

Teaching positions had to be filled by Colombians who were trained not only in pedagogy but also in biblical principles. Most of the Bible institute students were from river areas that had been evangelized by both missionaries and Colombians using the river launch years before. As it became possible, schools were started in more and more remote settlements. Eventually schools were established in extremely remote areas where none of the children had an opportunity to learn to read. Those rural teachers had a heart to bring God's truth to their communities. Often, beginning teachers would go to the rural areas with only a promise that the village people would provide them a place to sleep and something to eat. Because of the extreme poverty, these rural people could not provide any other amenities. They could not afford to pay the teachers a salary.

Along the rivers, crops could be planted and grown three times each year. However, it was rare for more than one crop to be harvested because of the problem of flooding. So these people had little money. Generally their crops would just be enough to meet their needs for food. The food they provided for the teachers was simple food like beans, rice, and fish. But the villagers were willing to do all they could if their children would receive some education and learn more of God's truth.

When I visited the villages to help or encourage the teachers, I would do my best to blend in with the people and be thankful for whatever they provided in the form of sleeping quarters and food. I ate many "interesting" things, knowing it was the best those villagers had to offer. No matter, I was always blessed with the hospitality and love shown by the rural Colombian Christians.

The young teachers were my pride and joy. These passionate young adults reminded me of the enthusiasm Paul and Stephen had for spreading the Gospel as it is recorded in the Book of Acts. They were willing and ready to go to areas that had no knowledge of the salvation God offers to them. It was more important to those teachers to spread the love of Jesus than to worry about how to improve their personal circumstances.

When the rural people came to a saving faith in Jesus Christ, they experienced whole-hearted conversion. Their beliefs were their guiding light when they lived in areas where they have little more than what they produced or made. They understood the concept of a supportive Christian community. It made no difference how humble their homes, they made a stranger feel welcome and feel as if it is a real blessing for them to share with the visitor. They had a love toward others that resulted in generous hospitality. They were a humble but loving people. The Christians in the remote areas did not have many material possessions, but they were giants in spiritual matters. They had a faith that was astonishing. This seemed to hold true even if they lived in an area where they were separated from other believers. Christians in the rural areas of Colombia were hidden treasures.

I visited the Gold Museum in Bogotá and saw beautiful beads that had been made by the indigenous people. Those beads were unearthed during archeological digs. One day, Luis, a Christian worker from an isolated area, brought me some little stone beads just like the ones in the museum. I immediately questioned him as to where he had found them. His reply was that a person in one of the remote villages gave them to him. They were hidden treasures, just like the rural Colombian people.

*****

Millie's insight: A jewel may be a precious stone, but it is also used to denote a treasured or highly valued person. Hidden along those remote river villages are hundreds of treasured and highly valued people who have been used by God to change darkness into light.

CHAPTER NINE

On Fire

"For Christ's love compels us, because we are convinced
that one died for all, and therefore all died. And he died for
all, that those who live should no longer live for themselves
but for him who died for them and was raised again."
2 Corinthians 5:14–15

*****

Millie's insight: Christian Colombian youth from rural areas
had the same spirit as Paul. They were compelled to preach the
Gospel. Woe to us if we as Christians do not preach the Gospel.

*****

Not long after I started working at the Peniel Bible Institute, I
developed a real feel for working with the Colombians. While
living in Medellín, I had worked with Colombian Christians on
the weekends and during the summer months; however, I was
always somewhat insulated from the people. I lived in the
mission compound, I worked with the children of missionaries,
and I associated with other missionaries.

Yes, when I moved to the Peniel Bible Institute campus, it
was still a mission compound. But there was a huge difference.
It was only a stone's throw away from the small rural village of
Cristalina, and about a hundred Colombians were housed on
the campus with us. Many of the modern conveniences were
there, but many were not. We had running water, bathrooms in
our homes, and electricity. However, things found in the cities
such as markets, buses, and shopping centers just were not

available. As I reflect about my work for the Lord in Colombia, I believe I started to work effectively with the Colombian people when I began my assignment at the Peniel Bible Institute. I was not insulated from the lives of the people. I was right there with them.

The spiritual fervor of the Christians who attended the institute—especially the ones who came in from the remote rural areas—never ceased to amaze me. God had given them a burning passion for evangelizing. It was something that happened to them after their conversion that was almost inexplicable. They were driven to get the message of salvation through Jesus Christ to their people, especially those living around their home area. But it didn't stop there. These zealous young people would seek out areas where they could take God's Word even if they had to take canoes up narrow rivers or tramp through jungles.

They had a Spirit-filled urgency to tell others about God's love for them. Its fervor could only be explained as a profound love for and commitment to Jesus. This urgency to share their faith with others was not produced by the teaching at the institute. The institute was just a training opportunity and an opportunity to learn more about the Bible. When they arrived, the Holy Spirit had already placed the desire to evangelize in their hearts. They were being obedient to the call. These young adults were full of energy. They ranged in age from 16 to late 20s, and most were single. Sometimes a young couple or a family with one or two young children did enroll.

It was impossible for those on-fire Christians to sit on that hill in the compound all weekend. They were young, had lots of energy, and felt drawn to let others know what Jesus had done in their lives. Lost souls were in need of being saved. So Friday afternoons, I would watch little groups of students heading out to witness. All along the train tracks, the students went to little towns to spread the Gospel. It didn't seem to make a difference to them how far it was or what they might face. And they did risk personal danger as that was still in the time of persecution against the Protestants, as those who opposed us labeled evangelical Christians.

Just like in the United States, one way to get involved in the surrounding community was through a sports program. In rural Colombia, that sport was soccer. The Bible institute campus had plenty of room for a soccer field, so hosting soccer games developed into not just a recreational activity but also a ministry. Students invited people from close-by villages to play. One or more games were played almost every Saturday on that field. Teams from neighboring communities descended on the grounds. Sometimes, teams were formed on the spot, and spectators divided so both sides had people cheering for them. We had our cheerleaders too. As a matter of fact, I gladly served as a cheerleader for whichever team needed one.

The small village of Caracolí had been involved in some of the soccer games with the students. I traveled to that little village, not just as a spectator, but also as a missionary to spread the Gospel. On one particular venture to Caracolí, we took a movie projector with us. The plan was to show a Christian movie, using sheets hung in the village street as a screen.

As we went into the town, we had no idea how the showing of the movie by evangelical Christians would be received. At other times when the students had gone into that same village to witness, people had thrown rotten tomatoes and rotten eggs at them. As some students made preparations for the movie, others went around town, passing out tracts.

God had worked in the hearts of two businessmen. While we were figuring out the logistics, a local shop owner said we could plug our projector in at his store because he had a generator that would ensure we had power if the time for the town's electricity to be turned off came before the movie was finished. It was an excellent location for us to spread God's Word because local farmers would bring their produce to town on Saturday evening so they could have it there to sell during the Sunday morning market time.

Another businessman decided to close the theater doors for that evening. He said he would let us use the theater, but it was not big enough. He offered to place his theater screen in the middle of the street. It worked very well because the projector projected on the screen in front, and in back, people watched a smaller version as it was projected on a wall behind us. It was a surprise to me that the image was sent backward as well as forward. And this time, it was a blessing because God used it to allow more people to be exposed to the Christian content of the movie. The village people were open to the Gospel that night. After the movie, the students passed out tracts and witnessed.

The next day, the store owner told us to plug our microphones into his outlet and to use the steps in front of his store for our morning worship service. The village street was a busy place. We were astounded that the businessman encouraged us to use his property during the profitable Sunday morning market time. On that visit, the Peniel Bible Institute students had brought a little singing group, a student to present the message, and many tracts explaining God's plan for salvation.

Just as we started to worship, the mass at the local Catholic church, which was only two doors down, let out. Now normally, that would be a concern. What kind of trouble would start?

But instead of trying to stop or interrupt our service, the villagers peacefully listened. No eggs. No tomatoes. Nothing. It seemed that practically everyone in the village came to learn about Jesus during that Sunday morning meeting. The timing of the service we held that Sunday morning was perfect. God honored the obedience of the students and gave us a tremendous time of spiritual and physical healing. Over and over, God worked in miraculous ways through those faithful young adults.

God called the Peniel Bible Institute students into ministry, and they actively practiced their faith. Their faithfulness and commitment to the Lord was often evident during times they were at the altar praying. One convicted student might stand up and give a testimony. Another might go to a fellow student or a teacher with whom they had been having difficulties to ask forgiveness.

I remember one time when a young man stood up just before a communion service was to begin. This was not uncommon because the Colombian Christians are very strict about taking communion. They will not participate if they are harboring ill feelings toward another person. This young man explained that he did not have a problem with any of the other students, but he was convicted by his own sin. He told how he had set aside some money as a tithe, which he planned to give when he came to the institute. He had not given it. He knew God was unhappy with him for not following through on his intentions. This young man asked that we wait until he could go to his room to fetch his money. He would not take communion until he had given his tithe.

At the end of their four years of study at the Bible institute, some of the graduates went out without any promise of a salary. They went in faith. Many times, the believers in an area agreed to give the ministers or teachers a place to sleep, and they took turns feeding them. This help for teachers continued for many years until Compassion International started helping with finances to educate rural children.

Compassion International was working in Haiti, and one of the missionaries in that program was the brother of the field director for OMS Colombia. The Compassion representative for Latin America expressed to his brother in Haiti that he wanted to expand their reach into Colombia and wondered if he knew anyone who might be interested in operating the program there. So in November of 1973, a contact was made. Compassion International visited Colombia. They observed six different schools in the river area and decided to begin giving scholarships to the children in those schools. This meant money was made available for salaries and the purchase of supplies for teachers and children in those impoverished areas. What a blessing and encouragement for those dear committed Christian teachers!

One year, the Peniel Bible Institute students decided they wanted to send one member of their group out as a missionary to Colombia, their own country. They decided to send a student into an area where there had been no evangelism. The students prayed together, selected a couple of students as possible missionaries, and then made a decision. The student they selected was one who never lost an opportunity to witness about his Lord and Savior. Bernabé was on fire for the Lord and excited to be their missionary.

When Bernabé arrived at the village selected as his mission field, he could not find a place to rent, so he slept on the park bench. Over time, he was able to win the people's hearts. He had a tremendous ministry during the year he was a missionary in their midst.

For a few years, the students sponsored one person in their group as a missionary. During the school recess time, their missionary would be sent to evangelize an area that had not heard the Gospel.

I was inspired by the commitment and spiritual faith of the young people who attended Peniel Bible Institute.

*****

Millie's insight: When Jesus saw the multitudes, he had compassion on them. Compassion compelled those new converts of the early church to take the Good News of salvation to those who walked in darkness. Do you have compassion for the multitudes around you who do not know Christ?

CHAPTER TEN

In the Line of Duty

"Have I not commanded you? Be strong and courageous. Do not be terrified; do not be discouraged, for the LORD your God will be with you wherever you go." Joshua 1:9

****

Millie's insight: God provides transportation, protection, housing, and companionship for accomplishing his work. Jesus provided food for the 5,000. God provided protection for Paul and the others during the shipwreck. How could God not provide for my needs and protect me?

*****

Felipe was a Christian worker that I remember well, mostly because of the memorable experiences we had on a trip to the Christian schools and congregations in the rural areas of Colombia where he ministered.

After some time of trouble, many of the little Christian schools in some areas had to close. Conditions had improved somewhat, so OMS would be able to assist teachers and pastors in opening them again. Therefore, I was making a trip to assist those teachers.

I was traveling by myself, and I was a bit apprehensive

because I knew very little about the area where I would be traveling. Making the transportation connections was my concern. I had no desire to be stranded in unfamiliar territory. My fellow missionaries and my Colombian friends who knew the area well assured me that I would be able to safely travel there even if I had little knowledge of the region. The transportation system to my destination was fairly easy to navigate. But, it was the rainy season.

This was not a trip on which I would be taking only a small traveling suitcase. I would also be taking boxes of textbooks and salary money for several of the teachers. This luggage would be a challenge for a large man, but it was an enormous concern for me as I only weighed about 100 pounds.

I was to travel on a train from Medellín until I reached the end of the line, arriving at about 3:00 p.m. At that point, transportation would be available to take me to the small port town of Tamalameque. I was told there would be plenty of time to catch a boat to El Banco. Two single missionary women working with another mission organization had been ministering in that port town for several years. I would spend the night with them and then proceed to the first village school I planned to visit. Again, they told me I did not need to worry.

The train traveled through mountainous country. During the rainy season, it was not uncommon to come upon landslides where large areas of dirt and rock gave away under the weight of the downpour. The muddy, rocky debris had to be removed from the tracks before the train could proceed to its destination. Sometimes the train crew was able to clear the way, but sometimes they had to wait for help to make the tracks passable.

The train, which under normal conditions would have arrived at the rural train stop close to Tamalameque by 3:00 p.m., did not arrive until 7:30 p.m. By this time in Colombia, it is pitch dark. I disembarked. I saw no bus, so I inquired about one. No more buses were available that night. The only way to reach the town of Tamalameque was by vehicle. All I saw were the train station and a couple of beer joints. I was standing there at the station with my suitcase, boxes of books, and the salary money. I frantically thought, *What am I going to do?* So I asked if there was anywhere around close where I could stay. I was told no.

A truck was parked close by. I approached the truck owner and asked him if he was going to Tamalameque. The driver answered, "No, but if you want to pay for an express trip, I will take you."

I inquired further, "If I go to Tamalameque, will there be a place I can stay for the night?"

"Oh yes. There are lots of places along the riverbank where you can stay for the night. That will not be any problem," he replied. Because no other viable options were available, I trusted him and made arrangements with him. Five people had exited the train at the same time that I did. One couple noticed I was making arrangements with the truck owner, so they drifted over and listened to the conversation. They asked if they could go too. The truck driver was very eager to have them ride along. The man asked how much it would cost. The driver responded, "Oh nothing. She is paying."

I thought, *At this point I do not care. I am not staying here for the night.* The couple crawled into the back of the truck while I road in the cab. By the time we reached Tamalameque, it was beginning to sprinkle. I wondered what I would do. I had these books that needed to be in out of the rain.

The truck owner let me out at the entrance of a store that was located in the front portion of a house. I went into the little storefront and asked where I could find a place to stay. "Oh, everything is closed now," came the quick reply.

I thought, *Nothing!* Immediately the Bible passage relating when Mary and Joseph were told there was no room in the inn came to mind. My next thought was, *Oh, Joseph and Mary, I know how you must have felt—except I am not pregnant. Thank heaven!*

I told the storeowner that I was on my way to El Banco and I wondered if there was a chance that a boat might be traveling there that evening. The owner assured me that no boats would be leaving until morning. Again I asked, "Is there nothing open where I can find a room to stay for the night?" Again the owner said there was nothing. I looked around and saw a bench just inside the shop door. So I asked, "There is a bench. May I just put these boxes in here and sleep on the bench?"

Again he refused. But he must have begun to feel sorry for me because he made an offer. He said, "I am beginning to fix a room to rent out. I have the walls up and the roof on but no flooring installed. I will put a tarp on the floor for you to lie down on, if you want." He also told me he did have a lock for the door.

I agreed to the conditions, but to ease my mind, I asked, "Now, there will not be anyone else in there with me, right?" He said there would not. So I went into the little building with my books and things. I would sleep in my clothes that night as often I did when in the rural areas. Just as I was ready to lie down and get some rest from the exhausting trip, a knock came on the door. It was the owner.

He said, "There was a lady who came in on the truck with you. She is wondering if she can come in and sleep too."

Because she had been with a man, I asked, "Is it just the lady?" He assured me that it was just her.

The woman had been in the room with me less than five minutes when someone pounded on the door. She hopped up about as fast as anyone can hop up. She opened the door, and the man came in with two big bottles of liquor. I thought, *Oh my goodness, here I am. I have this money on me. I have these books. I am alone. They have two full liquor bottles. What do I do? I don't know what to do in this situation.* I don't usually just open my Bible and read whatever passage is on the page. I am more purposeful in my Bible study. But that night in that circumstance, I turned on my flashlight and let my Bible fall open. My flashlight centered on this verse: "Have I not commanded you? Be strong and courageous. Do not be afraid; do not be discouraged, for the LORD your God will be with you wherever you go" Joshua 1:9.

I eagerly read it again then said to myself, "Okay, Lord. I must fear not. I must be courageous. You will be with me."

I placed the money I was carrying underneath my outside clothing. I wrapped the strap of my purse around my arm and used it as a pillow. Then God brought a verse to my memory. It was a verse missionaries had used a few years earlier when our mission compound was under a threat of attack while all the men were gone. Before the women went to bed that night, God gave them this verse: "In peace I will lie down and sleep, for you alone, LORD, make me dwell in safety" Psalm 4:8.

Amazingly, I quickly fell asleep and slept soundly until 4:00 the next morning. I awoke alert and rested. The couple was sound asleep. So I quietly gathered my belongs, left that building, and headed for the riverbank.

I swatted mosquitos and patiently waited for a motorboat that was going to El Banco. Finally, a boat arrived that was taking passengers. I was the first one to board it. Just as I was getting into the boat, the couple came out from the building where we had spent the night. They told me that I needed to take a different boat because it would take express people. I replied, "No, I have already made arrangements." It just so happened that there was not room for them in the boat I had hired. I was not going to let them manipulate the situation again so I would end up paying their way.

The missionary women at El Banco were very surprised to see me. They questioned, "Are you really going to continue your trip alone?" I had entertained no thoughts of turning back.

I replied, "Girls, what are you worrying about?" We all had a good laugh. These two gals were out there in the rural areas and traveled all over in their Jeep. They, like me, often traveled alone and in challenging areas.

I boarded a boat the next morning to travel to the first village on my itinerary. By afternoon, I was able to visit with some of the parents. To my surprise, they were very upset because the teacher was letting their kids out to play. I inquired as to when the teacher was doing this. They told me that about the middle of the morning the children always were outside playing. They said, "We send our kids to school to study—not to play."

I realized that these parents had never experienced a day of school. They had no idea how much work studying is. They did not understand that what the children were doing in the classroom was far more taxing than just sitting under a shade tree. So I patiently explained that the children needed some time to get some of the energy out of them so they could concentrate better on their studies. It was a profitable time for the parents and for me.

Felipe, the pastor of the OMS-related church in that village, and his wife prepared supper for me. As we sat down that evening, Felipe said he needed to visit some of the congregation, and he felt I needed someone to travel with me on this trip. I knew Felipe did not make enough money for him to have extra funds to purchase passage on the boats, and my funds were not overly ample. But I was not one to doubt the Lord's provision.

"Lord, if this will help him make contact with his congregation and other churches, I know you will provide," was my prayer. So Felipe and I started our trek the next morning.

When the first segment of our trip ended, Felipe and I disembarked from the boat. We had to wait for some time before a boat going in the right direction would be available. So we found a location where we could leave our luggage and the boxes of books. To pass the time, we started walking down the path in that little river port town. We passed by some children playing soccer, and we walked past some little shops that sold various items.

Suddenly, someone came running up behind us, calling, "*Seño! Seño!*" This is the word used in the river areas for *señora*, which is the title for married woman. Felipe told me to not turn around. He did not know who was calling. I was obviously a foreigner. My complexion and hair color were far too light for that area of Colombia. I did as instructed, but Felipe turned to face the person. It was a 15-year-old boy. He told Felipe that his mother sold bread and coffee in a shop back down the path. He said, "She wants to talk with you." So we turned around and proceeded to the little shop.

The lady offered us something to drink and some of her bread. We soon learned she would go home in the rural area that evening, make bread the next day, and return to town to sell it the following day. That was the way she made a living for her and her son. At that point, Felipe and I both realized that her son had been one of the children playing soccer as we walked down the path. She wanted to tell the story of what had happened in her son's life.

She told us that when her son was 5 years old, they were in the town of Magangué. Bill Gillam, an OMS missionary, and Pedro Gutiérrez, a Latin American missionary, were holding evangelistic meetings there. At the close of one of the services, Don Pedro gave an invitation for those who wanted healing to come forward. They anointed those people with oil and prayed for healing.

That little 5-year-old boy got up and went to the altar on his own. Don Pedro was moved because the little boy was walking on the outsides of both of his feet, which were severely deformed. When he was born, his feet were completely turned toward the inside. Don Pedro asked that brave little boy if he had come alone. The little boy replied, "No, my mother is back there." As Don Pedro looked up, he saw his mother starting down the aisle. The young boy told his mother that if God healed him, he wanted to serve God. They knelt, anointed him with oil, and prayed for him. It didn't happen all at once. But within days both feet gradually began to be corrected. As we saw the kids playing soccer earlier, we would not have imagined that youngster had been born with such a debilitating deformity. He walked, ran, and played just like the others. The only treatment he had received was God's healing touch.

I was able to confirm the story of the healing of that boy with the deformed feet. Several years later, my husband Vernon needed additional training in Spanish, so he enrolled at the language school in San José, Costa Rica. During the time we were there, Vernon and I attended a church where Don Pedro Gutiérrez was the pastor. He remembered that boy and the prayer for healing in Magangué.

During the remainder of the trip, my heart was touched by the dedication of the teachers. They had no textbooks for the children, and many of the children had no writing materials or notebooks. Yet the teachers worked hard and effectively at instructing the children. They put their hearts, energy, and love into giving those children an education. It was clear to me, as I worked with and helped these rural teachers, I was not only helping the teachers and children, but I was also helping the congregations.

God provided when he sent Felipe with me on that trip. And miraculously, I was able to pay for all of Felipe's transportation expenses. God stretched the money I had for covering only my expenses to covering the expenses for both Felipe and me. The pesos stretched and stretched and stretched.

*****

Millie's insight: When we put our trust in God, he will supply all our needs in Christ Jesus.

Wedding photo of Millie's parents,
Howard and Melita McCary

Five-year-old Millie

Vernon (l) with his brother Jim
and sister Elsie

71

Millie's family in 1937: Millie (front); sisters Pearl and Margie (middle l to r); father Howard, mother Melita, brother Wayne (back l to r)

Millie (r) in a school play during her freshman year at Friends University

Millie graduated from Friends University in 1953.

72

*George Washington School
children in 1956 (Medellín)*

*Children's choir, directed
by Millie, at Amador
Church in Medellín*

*Children's concession stand at the first World Vision Pastors' Convention in
Medellín. The proceeds were given to Bob Pierce to help orphans in Korea.*

73

CHAPTER ELEVEN

Victory in Spite of Evil
Joy in the Midst of Physical Danger

"… the God we serve is able to save us from it, and he will rescue us from your hand …" Daniel 3:17b

*****

Millie's insight: Satan uses evil forces to keep mankind in bondage, but Christ can loose those evil chains and free us from Satan's grip.

*****

I consider the Cardoza family as dear Christian friends, and I always enjoyed visiting them on my trips into the river areas. But one time, after we left their village, a dangerous surprise greeted my traveling companions and me.

Two Bible institute teachers, the dean of women, and I traveled to several villages where OMS had churches. Our purpose was to encourage young people to open their lives to the Lord's leading. We were searching for those who, with a little encouragement, would attend the Bible institute to prepare for full-time Christian service.

After visiting a couple of schools, we prepared to travel to the next destination. We needed to get an early start. Because in the river areas they generally do not have an early breakfast, we left without eating. We expected to board one of the first morning river launches. That did not happen. After waiting for some time, we searched for a place to purchase breakfast. Finally, we found a little place that sold demitasse cups of coffee.

Colombians brew a strong coffee drink. To make that little cup, they used a similar amount of coffee beans as would be used in a fairly large coffee maker in the U.S. In addition, they dissolved as much sugar as they could in that small amount of liquid. My missionary friends and I often joked that a spoon could stand on its own in one of those cups of coffee.

Our group of four expected to leave soon, but we waited and waited and waited. Nothing came along. Colombian men are used to having a large breakfast. True, they did not have a wide option of foods. They ate what was available. Even though it might not be the most nutritious, breakfast was always a large meal. Then they ate a light evening meal. Needless to say, the two men with us were famished. When a small canoe with an outboard motor finally appeared in the late afternoon, we were all hungry but ready to get on with our trip. We boarded.

The farmers along the rivers often raised cattle and made cheese. The cheese they make is similar to cottage cheese, but it is solid and very salty because they use salt for a preservative. They cut pieces off the large cheese slabs to eat.

The river was relatively narrow. It was somewhat dangerous because of floating debris and alligators, but we did not take notice because our stomachs were empty. The men were desperate for food. As we passed the farms, they called, "Queso? Queso?" No answer came, and on we traveled. Eventually, someone answered back that yes they had cheese. So we disembarked. Unfortunately it was in an area that made the landing difficult.

Once we were on shore, we were glad to stretch our legs, and we all walked to the farmhouse. The farmer had a big slab of white cheese. The only thing I could think of was the times I had been up and down the river and saw men on the river launches with their feet propped up on a large slab of the unwrapped cheese. That memory and the saltiness of the cheese deterred both Celina and me from purchasing some. We had no drinkable water, and the river water was contaminated with the sewage that emptied into it. The men did not care. They were hungry.

The farmers also make large balls of crude sugar. They boil the sugar down and form a ball of solid sweetness. When eating the salty cheese, they knock off some of the sugar to eat with the cheese as that helps neutralize the salt. But like the cheese, it also increases your thirst because it was pure sugar.

After we boarded the canoe and headed down the river, of course, the men became very thirsty, so they drank the river water. I feared they would become sick while on the trip. Both of those men knew of the dangers of drinking river water. One of them was from the area and probably had some immunity to the germs populating the water in that location. It was only by God's grace that neither became ill.

We arrived at Colorado at about 1:30 in the morning. We were tired, hungry, and about ready to drop. What a blessing! We knew all we had to do was go to the hospitable Cardoza home to have a place to stay overnight. They would provide relief from our long travel ordeal. This wonderful, strong Christian family always welcomed Bible institute missionaries who visited. The Cardoza family did not have a large house, but it was the largest in the village. They needed the space because they had 10 children.

Mrs. Cardoza was thrilled to see us. She immediately insisted on fixing something for us to eat. They had the only oven in the village. It was an outdoor earthen oven made of mud. When baking bread in that earthen oven, she started by burning wood in the oven until it was very hot. Then she placed the dough on a slab and baked it. The bread absorbed the wood flavor. Delicious.

Mrs. Cardoza also prepared some hot chocolate for us. This area is in a hot climate, but at that hour of the early morning, the air was cool, and the hot nourishing drink was perfect. She made it by heating an unsweetened chocolate bar, crude sugar, and water. A little wooden ball contraption was placed in the chocolate mixture and spun until the drink became foamy. I don't think I have ever had a piece of bread and a cup of hot chocolate that was as satisfyingly delicious. That dear lady had joyfully interrupted her sleep at 1:30 a.m. to prepare a meal for us that she served at 3:30. Colombians normally start their day at 4:00 a.m. By the time we finished eating, Mr. Cardoza started waking the children. What a joy it was for my friends and me to arrive in the middle of the night like we did and to receive such gracious hospitality!

The church in that village had a difficult time building a structure. They would have the walls partway up, and the enemies would knock them down with large sledgehammers during the night. This happened several times, but the believers in Colorado were determined. Through perseverance, the building was completed. Years later, in 2012, they were even able to construct a large addition to their original structure.

When we were ready to continue our travels, our missionary group hired an outboard motor boat to go to the next location. It was a bit more comfortable than the narrow canoe.

The next destination on the trip was an entirely different experience. It had slipped our minds that we were traveling during the week before Lent. During this week, some of the communities held large parties. In the areas of the most extreme and more lawless influences, it could be quite dangerous. These areas were generally located in remote regions. The revelers were busy sinning to make up for the sin they would not be allowed to commit during Lent. The less civil individuals thought it was their right to commit any and all the sin they wanted. Because of the lack of restraint, I learned to be very cautious and purposeful in planning my activities the week before Lent.

By the time we arrived at the next location, the big fling before Lent was in full swing. My little traveling group first realized what time of year it was when we saw two or three dead bodies floating past us on the river. During the festival times, if a person ended up in the river, revelers didn't interrupt their partying activities to retrieve a corpse or to even save a drowning person. The body was left to float down the river. The victim might have wandered into the river and passed out from heavy drinking and not be able to save himself from drowning.

Or sometimes the revelers punished someone they did not like by rolling them around in the mud and walked off, leaving them to drown. Or maybe the person who was rolled in the mud was so drunk he continued to roll out into the river where the currents pulled him under.

During the first day of the festival week, people threw cornstarch all over other people as a common practical joke. That is not so bad because although the cornstarch might choke you, you can live through it. Sometimes, they mixed up a type of whitewash or threw paint on one another.

Another common practice was approaching people and demanding money so the partiers could buy liquor. Anyone who did not give them money was punished in whatever manner the partiers chose. When we entered the village, some men ran toward us ready to douse us with whitewash. One of the fellows looked at me and stated, "Oh no, she is already white." And they let us by.

Our missionary group made it to the house where we planned to stay. That family told us that the week's festivities where just beginning, and the situation was beginning to get bad. They strongly advised us to not go outside the house. For three days, we hid in that house behind bags of rice. Thankfully, the family had just finished the rice harvest, so we had an effective place to hide, away from the eyes of the mischief-makers. Once in a while, a member of our group emerged from our hiding place to get something to eat, as a household member kept watch at the door.

During the night, we could hear men screaming in pain and anguish. I was told the punishments used on a person who would not readily give the evil men money, or for that matter anything they wanted, were often very severe. During those nights, containers of biting ants had been placed in the trees. The uncooperative men were smeared with creosote. Then they were tied to the trees with the containers of ants. The containers were opened and the biting ants attacked the men. They screamed for mercy. It was awful.

Devastation caused by the pre-Lent mischief was not just from the cruelty inflicted during the week before Lent, but serious disease was caused from injuries and open wounds that were not properly treated. Tetanus was common since the water and mud were unsanitary because of the hog and cattle refuse.

Even though all that evil was going on outside the doors of the house of this dear Christian family, God was so good. The Christians in the village took extremely good care of us. They knew we could not walk through the village, so they gathered in the home where we were hidden away. It was very close quarters and brotherly communion. As a result of that visit, some of their young people came to the Bible institute the very next year. It was victory in spite of all the evil that happened.

That experience helped me better understand the young people who came into the Bible institute to study because I had experienced cultural influences of their village. After that threatening happenstance, I was very careful never to travel into remote areas during the week before Lent again. Later, I traveled to that village several times during other times of the year and felt quite safe.

*****

Millie's insight: God is able to protect us from the Evil One, and he will give us the joy of seeing people turn from their evil ways. We never know how God will work in the present circumstances.

CHAPTER TWELVE

Nothing Will Harm You

"I have given you authority to trample on snakes and scorpions and to overcome all the power of the enemy; nothing will harm you." Luke 10:19

*****

Millie's insight: When God leads us out, he tramples Satan under his feet. God goes before us and prepares the way.

*****

I am a bit shaky when it comes to snakes. I don't panic when I encounter a snake, but I do not want anything to do with them, even if it is a harmless garter snake. However, when visiting the rural areas, encountering snakes was always a possibility.

For years, OMS had a program called NOW Corps, which was designed to give college students an opportunity to spend the summer on the mission field. This program not only provided temporary workers, but it also helped students discern if they were called to the mission field. It offered college students a realistic missionary work experience and provided them with an idea of what living conditions to expect. In addition, the students had the experience of raising their own funds, just like career missionaries.

We tried to give them a broad-based experience. The students worked in the compound and the surrounding area. But they also accompanied us as we visited churches in the outlying areas. This allowed them to experience a variety of ministries operating on the mission field where they were volunteering.

I felt privileged when one or more of these college students was assigned to me. Sometimes, I oversaw a small group. Several times, I took these young people into the rural areas because I was traveling a lot.

One summer, Mary Speakman participated in the NOW Corps, and I took her on one of my river trips. She played the accordion well, so I gladly let her use my accordion as she conducted the song service during the worship meetings in the villages we visited. We divided the responsibilities. Mary was in charge of the song service, and I did the speaking.

At the second stop on the river, the unexpected happened. Like normal, the rural church building was made of bamboo stick walls, thatched roof, and dirt floor. A straight, long bench was the only seating. But that night, the villagers had brought in two chairs for us, their special guests.

The service had just begun when I noticed some people looking up at the roof. I wondered what was happening. About that time, the lay pastor rose and addressed the group. He said, "That snake is going to be okay up there. Just forget about it, and we will kill it after the service."

The snake would crawl a little way through the thatched roof, lean down a bit, and then loop back up. I watched it come closer to our location as it traveled along the middle of the roof. Just before it was time for me to speak, I whispered to Mary, "If that snake gets over my head and starts to loop down, kick me. I am not staying under that thing when it loops down."

During the entire time I spoke, I regularly took a quick glance at Mary out of the corner of my eye. I wanted to make sure that she was keeping a close eye on the snake. The snake did come rather close before the service ended, but it did not move right over my head. When the service was over and most of the people had gone, Mary and I moved over to the side of the building as the pastor prodded the snake with a long stick.

The snake fell to the floor. In a flash, both Mary and I hopped on the chairs on which we had been sitting. Neither of us squealed, but we both caught our breath, and our hearts were pumping extra hard.

In short order, the snake was killed. However, the conventional wisdom is that when you find one snake there is usually another one close by. And we were spending the night in a small building right behind the church. We wondered where the second snake was located.

The small building serving as our sleeping quarters did not have electricity, nor did any of the other buildings in the area. We made jokes and laughed as we conducted a thorough search of our sleeping quarters with our flashlights for a possible second snake. Neither Mary nor I wanted any surprises that night.

We placed our suitcases onto the ends of our beds because we did not want a snake to get into our belongings as we slept. We crawled under the mosquito netting that had been provided to go over our beds. After reading some Scripture, we prayed, thanking God for the good service that evening. Mary had just started to pray when she suddenly said, "Lord, excuse me. Something just hit my leg."

I quickly grabbed the flashlight and shined it on Mary's leg. It was the strap of her purse. We laughed so hard that we forgot to be too afraid.

Mary returned to the United States after her adventures with me that summer. She continued her education at Asbury University in Wilmore, Kentucky, where she met her husband Bob Sutherland. She and her husband served on the mission field in Colombia for several years and also a few years in Ecuador with OMS.

*****

Millie's insight: God must smile at times when we realize how quickly we forget he is always right there protecting us from harm.

CHAPTER THIRTEEN

Stop. Drop. Pray.
Praying for Missionaries

"As for me, far be it from me that I should sin against the
LORD by failing to pray for you." 1 Samuel 12:23a

*****

Millie's insight: If God lays it on your heart to pray for a
missionary, it is essential that you obey. That missionary most
likely is in a very challenging, difficult, or dangerous situation.

*****

As a young adult, I was not a daredevil. As a matter of fact,
people from my hometown would have considered me strong-
willed but timid. My childhood friends would have laughed at
the idea that I would ride through the Colombian jungle on a
mule with five men I had known only a few hours to a destination for which I had no guiding directions. But when God
called, I went.

I was working at the Peniel Bible Institute in Cristalina,
training Colombian nationals as teachers. The goal was to
prepare teachers to fill teacher vacancies in existing Christian
schools and to start Christian day schools in villages that had
no educational opportunities for the children. I served as coordinator of all the Colombian Christian schools started by One

Mission Society. One of my responsibilities was to travel to the remote villages to assist teachers in their efforts. Antonio, a recent graduate of the Peniel Bible Institute, was eager to set up a school in the small jungle community of La Virgin. I made plans to travel to that remote village to help this beginning teacher establish a school. Word had been sent to Antonio to meet me at the closest small river port on a specific date. From there, we would travel into the jungle to the village.

Final arrangements were made, and I traveled to the port town of Caucasia. I arrived on the designated day at the pastor's home where Antonio was to meet me, but he was not there. Antonio did not have a calendar, as calendars were irrelevant in that part of the country. Rural Colombians only needed to know what day of the week it was. He had dutifully arrived to meet me on the correct day—but the week before. Since I was not at the designated meeting place, he returned home and assumed I was unable to come at that time for some reason. He would wait word for a new date.

I was disappointed and felt that maybe my time and energy had been wasted. But I was not easily sidetracked when I believed I was on God's mission. I asked for directions to the village but was firmly told that I could not travel there alone, as I would not be able to find the way. It seemed that my only option was to spend the evening in the small river port and return to Medellín the next day. Nevertheless, I looked forward to worshiping God in the church OMS had established in Caucasia. I was not going to miss an opportunity to praise God with the Colombian believers. It would refresh my spirit.

As I entered the church, the pastor told me that three men from the village of La Virgin had arrived and would be in the service. They would be returning to their village the next day. I approached the men. They were willing to guide me. They suggested I stay in a room close to the port that night because they planned on leaving early the next morning. I trusted these three new acquaintances with my safety, as they were Christians. I rejoiced that God had provided a way for me to reach my destination so I could help Antonio establish a school for the children who lived far back in the jungle area.

The room by the port left much to be desired. But I was used to the idea that accommodations would be fairly primitive as I traveled in the rural areas of Colombia. This room was a bare-bones room, but it would be satisfactory for one night, or so I thought.

Everything was fine until the lights went out at ten o'clock. This was customary, and I expected the electricity to be shut off at that time. However, when the lights went out, the bedbugs emerged from every crack and crevice in the room. Previously I had learned that the best way to fight the bedbugs was to shine my flashlight on them. So I would doze until the bedbugs became unbearable, and then I would turn my flashlight on them. Because it was impossible to really sleep, I did not find it hard to be at the riverbank by 6:00 a.m.

Bedbugs were a notorious problem in rural areas. The bites cause uncomfortable welts on the skin. Apparently the body can became less sensitive to the bites and the welts seem to be less severe after continued exposure. The only way the rural people had to rid themselves of the bedbugs was to boil the straw mats used on their beds in a large pot. The bugs would float to the top and cover the top of the water. This process was a lot of work, and handling the scalded bedding was somewhat dangerous. The bedding had to be heavily infested before the villagers would undertake this task.

Even though the men had told me they would leave at 6:00 a.m., they did not leave until 8:30. I had learned that this was not an unusual occurrence with the rural people. They did not live by the clock. They could be delayed by any number of things. The most common reason, and the most important to them, was conversation with an old, or even a new, friend. My nine years on the mission field in Colombia had taught me to expect delays and to be patient.

The three men and I finally boarded a small aluminum boat with an outboard motor and headed down river. This boat had platform seats so when we reached the landing 1½ hours later, I was ready to stand up and place my feet on solid ground. We ate breakfast at the landing before starting the land trek. There is an old gospel hymn titled "Where He Leads Me I Will

Follow." After a few interesting culinary experiences, my missionary friends and I changed the title to "What He Feeds Me I Will Swallow." And that is what I did that day. I do not know what I was fed, but I gladly ate the meal.

After breakfast, the three men started leading me on a hilly trail. It was humid and hot. Before long, the men saw two neighbors coming their way with a pack of mules carrying produce to be loaded on a boat at the port landing. These two neighbors agreed that the three men and I could return with them on the mules after their cargo had been stowed on a boat. The men suggested I should wait for them at a nearby farmhouse. By this time, it was around 11:30 a.m.

The farm family was hospitable to me even though they did not know me. They enjoyed the wonderful diversion of hosting a visitor. They served me lunch and some excellent coffee. After lunch, I brought out a small battery-operated tape recorder and cassettes with Bible studies and gospel music in Spanish. I entertained the family with the tape recorder (which was considered amazing technology at that time) and witnessed to them. This was fun and enjoyable for the first couple of hours, but as the afternoon wore on, I began to wonder if the men and their neighbors were really returning that day or not. It was a huge relief when, at 5:30, the men returned.

The five men, two of whom were complete strangers (and I was not sure if they were Christians), started the trip into the jungle. I had been given a mule with a packsaddle. That may sound like a nice gesture, but after riding on it for several hours, I was not sure it was a blessing. You see, a packsaddle is a frame of two by four boards. The saddle was placed on a blanket on the mule's back. A couple of boards ran down the mule's back with A-frame boards attached at the mule's shoulders and hips. It was an excellent device for cargo but not exactly a comfortable seat for a human passenger. Nevertheless, I was not going to turn down an opportunity of riding instead of walking on the uneven terrain and in the humid heat. Nor was I going to be rude to the men who were graciously allowing me to travel with them.

I was glad to finally be heading toward my destination. The sun goes down in Colombia at about the same time year round—6:00 to 6:30 p.m. I assumed that the village would only be down the road a short distance as the men were eager to travel. I reasoned that if the village was very far the men would not have delayed their return to the farm for so long. Our small group was soon entering the jungle, and it would be too dark to travel since starlight and moonlight would be unable to penetrate to the floor of the jungle—or so I thought.

At dusk, I finally realized that we were not stopping soon. My mule was in the lead as we headed down the trail. The only people who knew where we were going were behind me. When darkness fell, I would not be able to see the trail. So I stopped and told the men my concern. They responded, "Don't worry. The mule knows the way. You are on the lead mule, so you must go first." So, with a deep breath to give me courage and a prayer to give me strength, I urged my mule down the path.

"Lord, am I in your will? Am I doing what you want me to do? I am scared. I hurt. I long to have this task completed," I prayed as I rode my mule through the jungle. I needed God's reassurance and peace. I had no idea how to reach my destination or how to return home. And worse than that, I was the lone female traveling with five men I had not known existed even a short 24 hours before.

The stars and the moon produced the only night illumination in rural Colombia. By this time, we were traveling through the dense jungle. Because the canopy of vegetation blocks most of the nighttime light, the darkness was intense. The small rays of light that did seep through the layers of leaves made vines dance like snakes hanging from overhead. Several times that night, I was sure a snake was going to land on my head or shoulders. The threat of snakes was real. To make it a bit scarier, I knew that many of the snakes in Colombia are venomous. The nighttime jungle noises can be quite frightening for someone who is not used to them. A novice cannot tell if the noises are from a carnivore that is dangerously close by or if they are far off and of no imminent threat.

Wildlife was not the only danger. Accidents in the dim light were always a possibility. At one point, the mule had to step up in a narrow area in the path. As it did, the saddle shifted some, and I could not make the necessary adjustment quickly enough in the dark. My leg was pinned between the wooden saddle and a tree. I wanted to yell out in pain, but did not. The whole lower half of my leg was black and blue for three weeks.

Fear gripped me. I was in the black jungle with snake-like vines dangling in my face, my leg had been crushed, I had no idea where I was, and five men I had just met were guiding me through an area known to be inhabited by dangerous creatures. Had I heard God's call correctly? Did he really want me here in this precarious situation? I prayed not only for God's guidance, but to calm my nerves. I was tired, hungry, and my body hurt. Why would God put me in this situation?

Finally, the men said we were stopping at a gate, which I could not see in the blackness. They explained that they needed to take some of the mules back to their owner. Four of the mules actually belonged to the three men with whom I had started the journey that morning. But the rest of the mules needed to be returned. The men said that I did not need to worry. They would be right back. That was very little comfort as I remembered the hours I had waited at the farmhouse earlier in the day after being given the same assurance. I desperately hoped their return would not be delayed. The wild animal noises seemed to intensify each moment I waited. Doubts and fears grew. I prayed for God's protection. Although it seemed like an eternity, this time the men really did return quickly.

We continued trudging through the jungle. My tired, aching body made me weary. I wondered how much longer we would be traveling through the night. How much farther could it be to the village? Finally, one of the men cupped his hands around his mouth and yelled, "Get up. The missionary is coming."

In a few moments, I could see small hand-held kerosene lanterns being lit all around the village. I had been unable to see it before. I watched the small flames from those lanterns as they were carried to the center of the cluster of huts. When we reached that group of village people, a chair with a cowhide seat was brought out to make my step down from my mule easier. By this time I had no feeling in my legs, and they would not support me. Fortunately, men standing nearby caught me and helped me to the ground.

I was told that I would go to a house close by where a woman was fixing supper for me. After that we would have a worship service. It was 9:30 p.m.! The food would be nice, but my body was exhausted and in pain. How would I ever be able to lead a worship service? Nevertheless, I prayed for the Lord to give me courage and strength. Much to my dismay, getting to the nearby house required that I walk across a log bridge over a little stream that washed refuse away from the village. Two kind men realized how shaky my legs were from the long mule ride. One man walked in front of me holding my hand and the other walked behind me holding the other hand. Those two men gently but firmly held my hands as I walked across the log. It flashed through my mind that Jesus was holding my hands. It was just like him to extend his helping hands in my time of need!

After the bowl of oatmeal, I felt better but still had little strength to conduct a worship service. That night, the recorded Bible studies and gospel songs on my cassette player were a blessing for both the villagers and me. After about two hours, the service ended. Two men helped me back across the log to a hut, which was used by the teacher. Rural people are hospitable and generous. Antonio had found other accommodations during my stay in the village.

The hut was small and was furnished only with a bed. The bed frame consisted of six poles pounded into the ground. The bed platform was about four feet off the ground. Split bamboo sticks were laid across the bed frame. It was covered with a white sheet, probably the only white sheet in this village. I am only five feet and one inch tall. To get into a bed that was four feet above the floor presented a challenge. However, it only took a moment for my practical mind to create a solution even though I was tired enough to have curled up on the floor. I knew the beds were placed that far above the ground for a reason. I turned my little traveling suitcase on end, grabbed the bed frame to steady myself, and managed to hoist myself onto the bed. At least I had protection from rain and a dry bed on which to sleep.

The next morning, as dawn approached, I heard voices outside my hut. Like the other huts in the village, it did not have a door. The men were heading out to work. They were whispering as they walked down the narrow path past the hut where I was sleeping. I could hear one of them ask, "I wonder if she is awake?" I called out to let them know I was. The men entered my hut and asked to hear another Bible study on my cassette player. They marveled at the battery-operated tape player. But the men wanted more than to see the marvelous machine again. They wanted to learn more about God. I happily started the tape player. Even though it was only a few minutes after 4:00 a.m., my heart warmed to see the men so eager to learn about our Lord and Savior, Jesus Christ.

The men then went out to work until 11:30. By that time the Colombian heat became oppressive. During the hot afternoon hours, villagers gathered outside their huts and sat in chairs or leaned against the poles of the huts waiting for the cooler evening air.

For three joyful days, Antonio and I worked together, setting up the school. We made lesson plans. We organized teaching supplies. Even though about 25 children lived in the village, none of them had ever attended school. They anticipated the first day with great excitement. No matter their age, they would all start in first grade.

My work in this little village was done. I assumed that one or two men would guide me to the river landing for my return trip. To my surprise, they showed up with a horse and a riding saddle. All of the village men gathered around the horse as I prepared to leave. I felt honored, like I was on *Queen for a Day,* a television program that was popular in the United States at that time. My entourage consisted of every man in the village, even the old grandfather. They walked out with me for the three-hour jungle trek. The village men were so appreciative. They could not stop thanking me. What a blessing for me to know God was using me in such a powerful way!

On this trip, I also planned to visit other remote areas. By the time I returned to the mission compound, I had been spreading God's Word and assisting teachers of small Christian day schools in the rural areas of Colombia for three weeks.

My mother faithfully wrote a letter to me each week. Three letters from her were waiting upon my return to Cristalina. I read the letters in the order my mother had written them. In the first letter, she started by saying she wished she knew what was happening to me on Wednesday. She had gone to her church in Wichita, Kansas, to dust and set up chairs for the prayer meeting held every Wednesday evening. As Mother worked, she felt a heavy burden to pray for me. She immediately stopped, went to the altar, knelt, and prayed. She prayed with such intensity that she forgot to watch the clock. She was unaware that she had prayed through the normal suppertime. My father went to the church, searching for her. He found her praying with intensity and realized she was praying for me, so he knelt and prayed. When the pastor entered the church that evening, he found my parents deep in prayer. The pastor joined them. As others arrived, they, too, joined in prayer at the altar. At about 9:30 p.m., my mother felt the burden lift from her heart. She stood up and sang the hymn, "Praise God From Whom All Blessings Flow."

They had been praying during the most dangerous and phys-ically difficult time of my travels through the jungle that night.

*****

Millie's insight: One of the important parts of the Great Commission includes Spirit-led prayer—being willing to pray when God speaks, when the Spirit moves in your heart, whether or not you know why you are praying, but knowing for whom you are praying. We fail the Lord when we do not pray when he puts someone on our hearts. Not everyone can go to the mis-sion field nor are they called to do so. However, all believers can promote the spreading of the Gospel to all nations through prayer support.

CHAPTER FOURTEEN

First Love

"Those who had been scattered preached the word
wherever they went." Acts 8:4

*****

Millie's insight: People who have been deprived from knowing
the truth about God for a long time come to faith with a hunger.
Their newfound experience with Christ makes them new creatures. They are encouraged for the first time in their lives and
want to share their faith with everyone.

*****

The small town of Galindo was one of those villages that became
almost completely Christian because of the believers' enthusiasm
for Christ. After they heard the Gospel, individual converts enthusiastically witnessed to their friends and neighbors. They could not
stop telling the Good News to other people.

The Peniel Bible Institute was started in order to encourage
this growth of faith in small rural areas such as Galindo. Rural
youth were trained to be teachers and ministers so they could
go back to their home villages or to more remote areas for the
purpose of spreading God's Word to the Colombian people.

Manuel's heart was for the people in the interior of
Colombia. His love for the Lord was evident as he studied at

the Peniel Bible Institute. I enjoyed working with him because of his enthusiasm. He was part of my Bible Quiz team, and he was also in classes I taught. Manuel was a true, on-fire, born-again Christian. After completing the coursework for the ministry program, he traveled to a remote village that was far beyond even the small village of Galindo to begin a new church. He ended up being both a minister and the teacher for that village's children.

Manuel received word that I was planning to visit Galindo. He wanted to visit with me, show me the ministry work he was doing, ask my advice, and pray with me. Manuel sent word to have the pastor in Galindo ask me if I would be able to travel to his village before returning to the mission compound because he would enjoy seeing me. When I heard of his request, I was thrilled to have the opportunity to witness his work and to visit with him.

One of the Galindo believers volunteered to take me into the interior. It was about a five-hour journey. I would have preferred walking, but my guide insisted I go on horseback. His desire was to make the trip as comfortable for me as possible because it was a long trip. Our plan was to travel to the village, stay overnight, and return the next day. I decided to leave most of my belongings in Galindo, as I would only need to bring a change of clothes and my overnight kit on this two-day excursion.

About 30 minutes from our destination, we had to cross a stream. Streams in the remote areas can be quite hazardous. Because I had not visited this area before, I had no idea what the normal flow and water level was for this stream. A rickety bridge went over the stream, and I wanted to use it. But my guide told me it was better to cross the stream on horseback. I trusted my guide for my safety.

The horse definitely did not want to go across the stream. Even though my guide repeatedly insisted he do so, the horse refused. Eventually he gave in. We had only gone a little way into the water when the horse started to swim.

I was terrified. I could not swim. I glanced up at the bridge, thinking that would have been better. But no. It had rotten and missing boards. The horse would not have made it across. As I looked at the stream bank ahead, a new terror gripped my heart.

The current had carried the horse and me down the stream. The opposite shore was not a nice gradual bank where the horse could easily walk out of the water. It was impossibly steep. It looked as if the ground went straight up.

I did not think the horse would be able to get on that bank, much less make the vertical climb to safety. Any attempt would surely result in a backward fall into the swiftly moving water. The frantic horse was barely keeping its head above water, and I was chest deep. What was I to do?

I grabbed hold of the saddle horn and clinched my feet into the stirrups as hard as I could. I held on for dear life and prayed, "Lord, give this horse solid ground on which to stand." The horse finally reached the shoreline and gave one big leap up the bank to solid ground. Somehow, my soaked body managed to stay on the horse. All that mattered was that we were across. My little bag with a change of clothes and my toiletries was completely waterlogged. But the horse and I had made it safely to solid ground on the other side of that rain-swollen stream. My guide had also safely crossed the treacherous stream, but he crossed on the rickety bridge.

Even though I was dripping wet and uncomfortable, I was glad to be traveling along a path again. As I rode those last few miles, I wondered how I was going to get my clothes dry.

I was still soaked when we arrived at the home to which we were traveling. It was a thatched-roof hut with split-bamboo walls and a dirt floor. What a relief for that trip to be over! Surely the stream would be back to its normal flow when the time came for the return trip.

Even though we had just arrived, we had no time to rest. A worship service had been planned, and it was almost time to begin. A 12-year-old girl looked at me with a worried expression. She said, "How are you going to be able to go to church that wet?" Then she ran into their hut and pulled a box out from underneath the bed. She found a dress and gave it to me to wear to church. At least my outer clothes were dry, and my hair was no longer dripping wet.

Even though Manuel had only been in the village a short time, he had an effective ministry. A small, enthusiastic group

97

of new believers and a good number of children were present. The children's school and the church services were held in a little thatched-roof, split-bamboo, dirt-floored hut that was almost identical to their homes. The rough wooden benches that decorated the interior of that crude building were where the children would sit for class the next morning.

That night after the service, this sweet girl and her family found a dry hammock and a blanket-like pad to help keep me warm during the night because jungle nights can be quite chilly. Though I had a dry dress and a pad to cover me, I was uncomfortably cold. Yet I was so thankful for the generosity of these village people and their willingness to make me as comfortable as they possibly could. The generous rural Colombian people taught me that hospitality is more than the condition of the facilities. It is being willing to sacrifice to make the visitor feel cared for and welcome. It is giving sacrificially for the welfare of another.

Needless to say, I did not ride the horse across the river on my return trip the next day even though the water level was much lower. I had an aversion to riding across that stream again. I preferred walking across the rickety bridge. I took care to not get my feet caught in its holes. Again, my guide crossed on the bridge, but this time he had a rope tied to the horse's halter as he led the horse across the stream, which had dropped to almost a normal water level. I rode the horse during the rest of the uneventful trip back to Galindo.

After a few years as a minister and teacher in that remote area, Manuel was able to attend seminary. This theological education was good preparation for the assignment he accepted as an instructor at the Peniel Bible Institute. In the mid-1980s, Manuel and his family moved to California, where he accepted a pastorate among Spanish immigrants. He has had a very successful ministry there.

The hospitality of the people of that remote village etched a lasting impression on me. They made every effort to take care of my needs and to make me as comfortable as they were able. Even though I experienced this level of generosity over and over in other locations, it never ceased to impress me and touch my heart. Those rural people who had so little would sacrificially give in an effort to make my stay with them a blessing. And a blessing it was—for both the villagers and for me.

*****

Millie's insight: Many of the young people who found faith in Christ strongly desired to share their faith and have Christian fellowship with other believers. To me, they seemed to be like the early apostles in that they could not stop talking about Christ, regardless of what happened.

CHAPTER FIFTEEN

God Will Provide

"God is not unjust; he will not forget your work and the love you have shown him as you have helped his people and continue to help them." Hebrews 6:10

*****

Millie's insight: When we are faithful to God, he will provide all we need.

*****

I was in the United States for a short, six-month home ministry assignment in 1963. Toward the end of this time, I traveled throughout Oklahoma and Texas with Ruth Bergert Messerschmidt, an OMS missionary friend. During the last trip we made together, Ruth warned me of the fate that was probably awaiting me. She said, "Millie, are you aware that if you return to Colombia for another four years, your possibilities for getting married are very slim."

I was already in my early 30s. By the time I would return to the United States again, I would be considered an "old maid." What a startling thought! Very few eligible men would be left, and the chances of meeting a suitable one would be miniscule. I gave an honest reply to Ruth's concern. "Ruth, I guess I've been so happy and busy enjoying every moment of my time serving God that I have not even thought of marriage possibilities slipping away. It is probably because of the fact that I am, first of all, dedicated to God, and then I am dedicated to the people he has sent me to serve. I'm last. Yet, God does supply everything we need. He knows everything I need." Little did I know what God had planned for me on the mission field for the next four years.

About 10 years prior to this time, God had already started arranging for me to meet the man I would marry. Vernon Young lived in Appleton, Wisconsin. He loved the Lord and had been asking God what he was to do with his life. Vernon graduated from high school in 1950. He knew that he would most likely be drafted into the Army and sent to Korea. If he was going to be called to serve the United States in the Korean War, Vernon preferred to be a part of the U.S. Air Force instead of serving in the Army. So he enlisted immediately after high school. Vernon worked while he waited to be called to active duty. In 1953, he began his military service.

During the time he was in Korea, Vernon saw thousands of Korean orphans. The plight of those Korean children was what God used to plant the desire to serve as a missionary in Vernon's heart. During his time serving in Korea, part of his military work required that he learn some Korean. Because he thought he would eventually be going back to Asia as a missionary, Vernon worked diligently to learn the language. After he returned to the U.S., he served in the Air Force Reserves from 1958-62 while he attended college.

Vernon knew God was calling him to the mission field, so he started studying Bible at Temple Bible School in Chattanooga, Tennessee. But he was unable to complete his course of study because his father was declared legally blind and requested that Vernon study at a university close to home so he could chauffeur his father and still earn his college degree. Vernon returned home to transport his father to work and wherever he needed to go as part of his daily activities. During this time, Vernon completed his teacher training course work. In 1963, Vernon graduated from Wisconsin State College in Oshkosh, Wisconsin.

Upon graduation, Vernon taught for two years in an intermediate school in Wisconsin. But during that time, he was continually looking forward to when he could begin serving God as a missionary. Vernon had talked with a friend of his parents' who was a staunch OMS supporter. The friend suggested that, because Vernon was a schoolteacher, he should consider applying for a position in Colombia as a teacher for the children of missionaries. OMS had recently announced an open position in Colombia for a person with his teaching skills and credentials.

In June 1965, after he was accepted for the Colombian teaching assignment, Vernon began raising his support. He was asked to attend the annual OMS missionary convention in Winona Lake, Indiana, because he could possibly gain some financial and prayer support there. This was the first OMS convention that Vernon had attended.

Something interesting happened. Vernon arrived a day early to the convention, and my parents also arrived a day early. When the missionaries arrived in those days, they had to get someone to help them build a little wooden booth for their displays. Vernon and my dad worked together, helping missionaries build display booths all that day. Both of them loved anything that had to do with carpentry. As they worked on those booths, they became acquainted with each other and developed a liking for each other. While the men were using their carpentry skills, Mother pressed all of the uniforms for the Seoul Korean Seminary Choir members who were to perform at the convention.

The following October, Vernon arrived in Colombia. The plan had been for him to teach at the George Washington School in Medellín, the same school where I had begun my missionary career. But of course, he had not met me yet nor did he know much about me, and I certainly did not know about him. However, a surprise came, as often happens when one is on the mission field. When Vernon arrived in Medellín, he was told that he would not be staying there as originally planned. He was to go to Cristalina, the location of Peniel Bible Institute. There he would teach four of the five Wittig children because no one in Medellín who could take on the children and no English-speaking school was available for them at Cristalina.

Vernon moved into a small dwelling next door to Mary Joiner and me. He was a quiet person. But anyone who observed him knew he was a true man of God.

Although Vernon took great interest in each of his school children, he paid special attention to the oldest Wittig boy, Johnny. Johnny had a bone infection called osteomyelitis. Vernon helped him in many ways. In the afternoons when class was over, Vernon took him to the shop and taught him woodworking skills. They often built projects together. Both the missionaries and nationals sensed Vernon's devotion to the Lord because of the way he approached any task he performed.

I realized that it wasn't only the people on the mission field who admired his devotion to God when I was able to read a letter written by a military chaplain in 1956. At that time, Vernon was in Korea. The chaplain serving his squadron recognized his devotion to God when he had to deliver the sad news that Vernon's brother Ben had passed away. The chaplain wrote a letter to the brothers' parents after he had delivered the sad news to Vernon. The chaplain wrote, "Vernon is one of our finest men. He is very faithful in his attendance at the chapel services, and he often comes to the chapel for his private prayers and meditations. He is one who sincerely endeavors to live as Christ would have him live."

This characteristic was clearly seen by all with whom Vernon had contact throughout his missionary career.

*****

Millie's insight: Many times when we don't understand some of the whys, we later do. God often meets us in the most unexpected places and at the most unexpected times, thus changing our plans for his plans. He does provide the places and times for us to be right there.

CHAPTER SIXTEEN

A Romance Begins

"If the LORD delights in a man's way, he makes his steps firm;" Psalm 37:23

"Wait for the LORD; be strong and take heart and wait for the LORD." Psalm 27:14

*****

Millie's insight: There is no need to worry about our future when God is leading us.

*****

Mary Joiner and I took a vacation trip to Panama in January of 1966. This was the first time since becoming a missionary that I took a vacation outside of Colombia. We had a great time. We were scheduled to return to Colombia the next morning, which was a good thing because we had spent almost all the money we had. As a matter of fact, we only had enough money to purchase an apple for each of us for our last meal in Panama. We laughed about having a scrawny meal of an apple. However, we weren't worried because we knew we would have a nice meal on the plane.

When we arrived at the airport the next day, we were bluntly told that the plane was overbooked. No seats were available for us. But they did provide a nice hotel for us to stay in until the next flight to Medellín. Actually, it was nicer than the hotel where we had been staying. They also gave us each three meal tickets. We ate more than an apple for our next meal.

When we arrived at Medellín the next day, someone informed us Vernon had hoped to meet us there and travel back with us to Cristalina. While we vacationed in Panama, he and Gene Wittig, director of Peniel Bible Institute, had taken a trip to Plan de Armas. When they returned to Cristalina, Vernon had some extra time and needed to make some purchases in Medellín, so he asked permission to travel to Medellín. His plan was to accompany Mary and me back to Cristalina. This did not seem a bit unusual, as missionaries traveled together whenever it was practical. Since we were delayed in returning, Vernon decided he could not justify waiting around in Medellín another day. So he left for Peniel Bible Institute. Mary and I left Medellín the day after arriving in Colombia. Our vacation was over.

Two days after returning from our vacation, Mary left with some of the Colombian faculty to interview prospective students for the next school year. I stayed at the institute to work on materials and to make preparations for the next school term. On a Thursday afternoon, Vernon came by and asked if I was going to the prayer meeting in the village that evening. While school was in session, we had services for the faculty and students on the compound. Since no students were around during the summer vacation time, we did not have church services at the compound and took the opportunity to pray and worship at the village church.

Again on Sunday, Vernon approached me as I started walking down to services. He asked if he could walk with me to the service. I think I was about as innocent as could be. I had no idea that Vernon was courting me. I thought he was just being nice. From that point on, Vernon often accompanied me to church services. As the summer weeks went by, Vernon started to talk with me about more than just the polite conversation topics that generally are common conversation topics between friends who work together. He started telling me about details

106

of his life. I started to know him as an interesting person and not just as a competent coworker.

It was during these walks to worship services in the village that Vernon related how the Lord had spoken to him about mission work. He told me how he thought that the Lord was probably calling him to Korea because of his experiences during the Korean War. However, as he and Gene traveled home, Vernon was prayerfully seeking a clear answer from God. He asked God if he was to be a missionary in Colombia or Korea. He prayed, "Lord, if you want me to stay in Colombia, make your will known to me." He had fallen in love with the people in Colombia. While in the middle of a stream, Vernon stopped, picked up a rock, and carried it to other side. As he crossed that stream, God revealed that he was to serve him in Colombia. It was only after Vernon was assured of this that he would allow himself to become more closely acquainted with me. Vernon sought to follow God's direction in all aspects of his life.

Our times of chats grew closer together. About the only place we could go was up and down the hill to church services in the village. Before long, we were always walking together to church or mission activities. Both of us knew the rules of the Peniel Bible Institute for having special friends of the opposite sex. Boyfriends and girlfriends were not to meet and talk at any location except the dining hall where the faculty could keep a watchful eye to ensure the behaviors were appropriate and honoring to God.

No one suspected Vernon and I had fallen in love, except Mary Joiner. It is hard to hide such a thing from your roommate and best friend. Vernon and I were very careful to not draw attention to ourselves. We would sit at the same table in the dining hall playing games with kids on Saturday and Sunday evenings. It never failed that we just happened to be at the same table but not necessarily partners. No one suspected our growing love for each other. They thought we were just good friends.

In May, after one of our walks back from the village, we decided to talk to Gene Wittig. It was becoming more difficult for us to keep our love for each other secret. We were sure of our love and that God had put us together. Since Gene was the person in charge of the mission personnel, he would need to bless our relationship before we could make it public.

Vernon arranged a time that we could talk with Gene. When Vernon told him we were in love and planning on getting engaged, he looked at us with a dumbfounded expression. Gene said, "I cannot believe this." He had no idea we had been courting for five months. His next comment was a question. "How did you do this without me knowing it?" Generally, Gene was the first to know about any developing romances among the students. He wanted to make sure the students were following biblical principles as their relationships developed.

We decided that it was best to keep our engagement quiet at the time. We talked about a possible wedding date in August. Several details would need to be resolved before it would be appropriate to announce an engagement. First, we would need permission from the mission, mostly for keeping the correspondence clear. Vernon had signed on to teach in Colombia for a two-year term while my agreement was for a four-year term. So Vernon's term would need to be extended two years. This was basically a concern about whether his support account could take that. God was good. As it happened, this concern was only a minor, easily resolved problem. His supporters agreed to extend their support for another two years. The people at the OMS home office knew both of us and were pleased when they learned about our engagement.

We both wanted our families to bless our plans to marry. My parents already knew Vernon from the encounter at the OMS convention. Vernon wrote a letter to them asking permission for my hand in marriage. Of course, they readily approved our plans. However, Vernon's parents didn't know me. We decided the best course would be for me to write a letter to introduce myself and to let Vernon's parents know that I absolutely adored their son. With this letter, we sent pictures in an effort to make them feel comfortable with our plans. What a surprise! Not only did we receive a letter from his mother, but we also received letters from all of Vernon's brothers and sisters. We were so excited. When we had the blessing of our parents, Gene agreed with our plans to travel to Medellín to announce our engagement there.

We made a surprise trip to Medellín. This trip proved to be an adventure as our train derailed three times that day. When the train finally arrived in Medellín, it was very late at night. We actually had to awaken the Brabon family with whom we would be staying. Margret Brabon rose and graciously greeted us. I had picked up a cold and was coughing. Because of my cough, she immediately surmised that we had traveled to Medellín for medical attention. However, it was not long before she noticed Vernon and I were holding hands. She gave us a funny, inquisitive look. Vernon quickly said, "Margaret, we have come up for a special meeting in the morning." Margaret was a bit confused at that point, as she knew nothing about a special meeting. Vernon, in his characteristically slow manner of speech, said, "Well uh, Millie and I are engaged." She jumped up quickly and said, "I have to wake up Harold! I can't take this by myself." Once Harold was up, she insisted on having a cup of tea to celebrate.

Immediately, Margaret began to make plans. She was just going to say we had a business meeting. The next morning, she sent John-Mark, their youngest son, around to tell people that they were to attend a meeting at 8:00 in the guesthouse, and it was important for all members of the missionary family to attend. Recently some conflicts had resulted over things being sent back and forth between the station at the Bible institute and the station in Medellín. For this reason, the missionaries thought they were being called to an important business meeting where a plan for resolving the issue would be shared.

Margaret started the meeting by saying, "Vernon and Millie have something they want to share with you this morning." You cannot imagine the surprised looks on the faces of those dear friends when Vernon, in his customary straightforward manner, said, "We came up to let you know Millie and I are engaged." The room exploded. One lady jumped up and down exclaiming, "You're engaged!" We had a great time with our friends, celebrating our engagement.

We did not stay in Medellín as we needed to return to the Bible institute. We decided on a little different approach for our announcement there. Vernon and I made a sign that read, "Mildred and Vernon are engaged." We walked into the dining hall one evening when all the students were in attendance for dinner and held up our sign. The students thought it was a joke. They talked among themselves afterwards saying they couldn't believe that we were really engaged. Vernon and I laughed heartily about the students' disbelief. Our courtship had been right before their eyes, and they had not seen it. We were living proof that a courtship following God's standards does not look like a courtship following cultural standards. Nevertheless, in the years ahead they would witness our love and devotion to each other as a happily married couple.

With the engagement announcements out of the way, we busied ourselves with planning a wedding for August 27. My mother and father had started the process of getting passports, and I was looking forward to having them visit me in Colombia. I was so disappointed when I received word in July that Mother had been diagnosed with colon cancer and would be having major surgery. She could not travel that summer. I was glad she elected to go ahead with the surgery and not delay it just so she could attend my wedding, although I knew it was a great disappointment for her. Vernon and I discussed getting married during our next HMA in the States. We wrote letters to both of our parents with that proposition. My parents responded immediately, saying they did not want us to put off our marriage. They felt we had waited long enough. They said they would celebrate with us when we were back in the U.S. So we continued with our plans for an August wedding.

We decided that since we were having our wedding at Cristalina, we wanted to invite the people from the village. All of the student body would be there also. Because the majority of those in attendance spoke only Spanish, we wanted the whole ceremony to be in Spanish. At that point, Vernon had not had any formal language training in Spanish. So we made a written copy of the vows so that we could memorize them. For me, memorizing the vows in Spanish was relatively easy.

However, for Vernon it was a very difficult process. He was determined and worked very hard to perfect what he was to say in Spanish. This would be the first Christian wedding that people from the village would witness.

We had fun planning the details of our wedding. Our mission field leader Burton Biddulph would officiate the marriage vows while our favorite Colombian pastor, Felipe Barajas, would give the message. Our attendants would be both American and Colombian. We decided to have three attendants each. Our flower girl and ring bearer would be Colombian.

I was fortunate because one of the students at Peniel Bible Institute was a talented seamstress. She embraced the project of making my white wedding gown. I showed her a picture of what I wanted for my gown and my attendants' dresses. She took measurements, and without a pattern made all the dresses.

As the wedding day drew near, we realized we had invited too many people to fit into our chapel. So we made plans for an outdoor wedding. This was a bit risky because an untimely Colombian rain could ruin our wedding plans. But we had very little choice. Our guests included our missionary friends, the Peniel Bible Institute faculty and students, people from the local town, as well as people from other villages that were relatively close.

About 10 days before the wedding, I baked my wedding cake and stored it in the freezer. One of my missionary friends helped me decorate it. A Scottish woman whose husband worked in a Colombian gold mine made other reception treats and decorations for us. OMS had a church in the village close to that gold mine. I visited that village several times and stayed in her home. One thing I will always remember about her is that she called her husband "old bloke." She was not a missionary—just a good friend. Often, she would come down and help us when we were having conventions. She happily prepared Scottish pastries and cute decorations for the wedding. She carefully packed them in a box that a missionary friend carried to the wedding.

The rain did come during the early morning hours the day of the wedding. It was a tropical downpour. The train carrying the seminary choir, the pianist, the song leader, and the bride's bouquet were caught on the other side of the river's overflow. My missionary friend who was carrying the box of Scottish pastries and decorations to our wedding was also on that train. At some point during the eight-hour rickety train ride, the box had fallen from the overhead bin. Some of the pastries and decorations were broken, but we were able to save enough to make out fine at the reception.

The train could not cross the rushing water. They would just have to wait until the water level was not so high and dangerous. Someone came to break the bad news to me. I was not about to let a little thing like a Colombian downpour spoil my attitude on my wedding day. With a twinkle in my eye, I said, "That's all right. We cannot go anywhere either. Vernon cannot run off now … he'll have to marry me." Finally, the train did make it through, causing only a bit of a delay for the wedding. The poor bride's bouquet was a bit wilted though.

The actual wedding ceremony was wonderful. Vernon transported me in a wheelbarrow from the wedding to the reception that was being held in the dining hall of the Bible institute. It was downhill all the way from the shade trees where we held the wedding ceremony. Vernon later asked me if I thought he would lose me as he wheeled me down the hill. I laughed and answered honestly, "Sure did."

Interestingly enough, Vernon and I made three moves during our first year of marriage. This is typical of missionary life. Vernon had his first trip to the river area that year. He had heard a lot about the river area; however, hearing about it and living among the people were two different things. We were gone about a week. His heart was broken for those people. That trip started a desire in both of us to move closer to a more remote river area to be able to minister to those people in a more effective way.

During the months of courting, as our relationship developed from respect, to admiration, to love, I thought back to the night I left the United States in 1954 for the first time on my way to Spanish language school in San José, Costa Rica. Mother had said to me, "It is so hard for me to see you go. I want you to go, but it is hard to see you go alone. Yet I know you are not alone. I know the Lord is with you." God was with me, and he provided a loving husband for me while I was on the mission field.

*****

Millie's insight: God provides in his perfect timing. God puts things together in perfect order at the appointed time. He leads us to the perfect place and gives perfect peace.

CHAPTER SEVENTEEN

A Dream Come True

"Be still before the Lord and wait patiently for him."
Psalm 37:7a

"I waited patiently for the Lord; he turned to me and
heard my cry." Psalm 40:1

*****

Millie's insight: Waiting periods are times of waiting upon
God.

*****

In early December of 1967, Vernon and I left for our first home
ministry assignment (HMA) after we were married. HMAs are
a very important part of the missionary's life. Periodically, we
return to the United States to visit with our supporters, prayer
warriors, friends, and family and share how God has been
working in our ministry. A very important part of that sharing
time is also raising support for so that we can continue on the
mission field. On a personal level, HMAs are an important time
to reconnect with family.

We thought we had everything perfectly planned. Through
my parents, I had made an appointment with a doctor that I had
used during an earlier HMA before I was married. This was a

very special appointment, as I wanted him to deliver our first child.

We flew into Indianapolis, Indiana, expecting that Vernon would leave early the next morning in an OMS car to drive to Appleton, Wisconsin, where his parents lived. We needed the Mission car for transportation, but the doctor had discouraged long car trips for me because I was close to my delivery date. So, I would fly most of the distance. Vernon would meet me at the airport in Appleton, Wisconsin, and drive the remaining few miles to his parent's home. I had corresponded with his parents but had not met them or Vernon's siblings. This was our first face-to-face meeting.

I was driven that afternoon by a member of the headquarters staff to the Indianapolis airport to board a plane and fly to Appleton. The plan was that the missionary using the car Vernon was to drive would return to Greenwood Saturday night, and Vernon would leave early Sunday morning. But often, missionaries, when traveling in the United States, do not make it out of a church service as quickly as we think we will, and that is what happened to her. So as I was being driven Sunday afternoon to the airport, Vernon was still waiting for someone to arrive with the Mission car. He knew this meant I would be meeting his family by myself. This was disappointing to him because he wanted to be there.

I was to deliver my first child in seven weeks, and soon I would be meeting my husband's family for the first time without him making introductions. Only prayer kept my anxiety under control. I would be meeting Mom and Dad Young, Vernon's seven siblings, their spouses, and all their children without Vernon by my side.

I met the whole clan. Once the introductions were over, Mom Young thoughtfully asked me if I had had anything to eat. Of course I told her no because I was in need of nourishment. So she sent Vernon's sister Elsie, who was still living at home, to the kitchen to prepare something for me.

I grew up on a farm in northwestern Arkansas. The only cheese I ate was the cottage cheese Mother made. I did not care for any other kind of cheese, as I really did not like the smell of

116

processed cheese. At that time, processed cheese was expensive in Colombia, so I had not eaten any there either, even though I had learned to eat almost anything while on the mission field. Now, I was in the cheese state of the United States. When I walked into the kitchen, I saw this large attractive platter with all kinds of processed cheeses and a few little crackers. I knew I had to eat and it was nutritious, and I was at the home of my mother-in-law whom I had just met. I ate the cheese. That was the beginning of my learning to love cheese.

The evening went on almost forever. We waited by the phone for Vernon to call with a report as to where he was on the road. The phone finally rang. Vernon's sister Elsie said, "Oh, I bet that is Ein."

Vernon's mother gave Elsie a strange look and exclaimed, "No. No, Elsie. We were not going to let that out." Just as all kinds of questions were running through my head, she turned to me and said, "Mildred, it's that, well that, we have always called Vernon by the name of Ein for Einstein because from the time he was just a young child he loved science. He carried rocks and everything you could think of into the house. But we made him put them in the attic. He would go into the attic and study his collections and go over all his science things. And they are still there."

They had promised themselves that they would not call Vernon by their pet name of Ein around me—especially in the beginning.

Vernon finally arrived. Everyone was on good behavior and called Vernon by his name. When we were settled in bed that night, I rolled over and said, "Ein." We had a great laugh when he realized I had found out about his family's pet name for him.

We flew from there to Wichita, Kansas, where my parents lived. On January 17, 1968, our first child was born. One thing about it, Colleen never had a chance to be shy. When she was 18 days old, we set out on the road to do deputation work. Since OMS is a faith mission, we are not supported by a denomination. We raise our funds through churches of different denominations, friends, and acquaintances. This means that the greater share of our home ministry assignment time is spent traveling, speaking in church services, participating in missionary conferences, and visiting at home meetings.

We traveled until December that year. We covered many miles—north to south and east to west across the United States. In her first year of life, Colleen quickly learned to smile when people approached her. When someone paid any attention to her, she always smiled.

In December 1968, we left for San José, Costa Rica, for four months so Vernon could attend language school. He wanted to learn to understand and speak Spanish better.

When we returned to Colombia, we hoped we would be able to move close to the river area in one of those port towns where we could be near the people with whom we were working. But we were still needed at the Peniel Bible Institute because Vernon and I were the only instructors for the teacher training courses.

Our second daughter was born in August of 1969. Joyce was born in a Medellín hospital. The first time I visited the office of our pediatrician, he put Joyce in his hand and took her out into the waiting room to show everyone her white, white skin and the bright red strawberry birthmark on her bottom. He said, "*Mire, mire. Que divino,*" which translates to. "Look, look. How divine." I do not think he had delivered a white baby before. That kind of birthmark does disappear as the child grows. But we still tease Joyce.

Colleen was 19 months old by this time. Her first language was Spanish. She understood English but spoke only Spanish.

When Joyce was about three weeks old, we had gone back to the Peniel Bible Institute in Cristalina. I was changing her bedding, so I put a pad on the concrete floor and laid her on the pad. As I was changing the bedding I heard Colleen say, "*Caballo, caballo,*" which translates to "horsey" in English. Colleen was on Joyce's back, riding her like a toy horse. Joyce quickly learned to live through the dangers of life with an older sister.

Because both of our girls played with the Spanish-speaking kids, they learned to speak Spanish first. This was not much of a problem as long as we were living in Colombia, but we knew we

118

would be on HMA in the United States someday. Vernon and I decided that at home we would speak only English. When we were outside our door, we would speak Spanish. It was quite obvious that the girls saw no purpose for speaking English. They would politely listen to what we had to say in English then answer us in Spanish. They absolutely refused to speak English.

As we were making our final preparation for our next HMA, I had given Joyce the task of taking our dog's dishes to the family who had graciously agreed to keep it in our absence. I heard her say with a very heavy Spanish accent, "Come, dog." Then she excitedly ran into the house, exclaiming in Spanish, "Mommy, did you hear me? I was speaking in English!"

Within two weeks after arriving in the United States, both girls were speaking English. If they didn't know the English word, they would insert the Spanish word in the middle of the English sentence just like it belonged there.

During the four years between our first and second HMA, Vernon had a chance to visit many of the rural areas. Our desire for moving to the river area became stronger and stronger.

In January 1974, we returned to Colombia and were asked to return to the Bible institute, as no one else was available to teach the pedagogy courses. One of the first things we heard was that Wally Erickson of Compassion International had been in Colombia the previous November and offered scholarships for six of our Christian day schools. These schools had student bodies of 50 to 100 students. OMS personnel in Colombia along with Wally Erickson had already decided that Vernon would be the director of Compassion International in Colombia. That was the first surprise after our arrival. The second surprise was that the OMS-related national church had named me as the coordinator for all of the Christian day schools. At that time, there were 13.

We were so excited. It was a perfect fit. Vernon could do the traveling and take materials to the teachers. I could do the office work, plan for in-service training for the teachers, purchase teaching materials, and many other such tasks. This arrangement would make good use of our time, energy, and mission resources. However, we were still living and teaching at the Bible institute. When Vernon was out visiting the schools, I taught his classes. We were very busy, and I was thankful for assistance from institute students who were willing to give a few hours to help with the housework and watching the children.

In March, we experienced the joy of the birth of our son Howard. He was born in a hospital in Medellín.

In January of 1975, at the annual business meeting of the Colombia missionaries, Vernon and I were commissioned to go to the river area to work. God had granted us our dream. We were not given an exact location to live, so we had to decide on a location. It needed to be a port village in a central location. We settled on Magangué, a village with a population of about 2,000. It was on the bank of the Magdalena River, Colombia's largest river, in the center of the area where our schools were located.

We would be responsible for working with the schools. Vernon had also asked to work with churches and pastors in the river area. He was granted that and encouraged to do evangelism. He could do all of that in addition to overseeing the schools because he would be visiting the villages anyway as a part of his other responsibilities.

I remember the day Vernon and I traveled to Magangué to locate a place to rent. We found what they called an apartment. It was actually living quarters on the third floor of a hardware store. The owner used the second floor as storage for excess items. Of course, the first floor was the hardware store itself. The living area was fairly large. It had four bedrooms with a floor plan like a house. The cost for renting the apartment fit into the budget that OMS had given us. This apartment also had a window air conditioner in one of the bedrooms, which was a recommendation of the mission leaders. The only real disadvantage to that apartment was the steps ... 47 of them! The kids perfected their counting skills using those stairs. We would count, "One, two, three, four ..." To answer the door, we had to go down those steps to the first floor where the exterior door was located. But, I was very thankful for the low sidewalls that extended up high enough around the edges of the flat concrete roof for me to allow the kids to play up there.

Actually, it was the view from the flat concrete roof that inspired Vernon and me. When we first examined the apartment, we stood holding hands, looking at the river. The view was magnificent. We could see the river's path in both directions. As we held hands, we knew this was the place where God was placing us to serve him.

The move was quite a step of reliance on God's provision. Any move with young children is challenging, and this one had its own set of obstacles. The girls were young, and Howard was not yet a year old when we moved to Magangué in January 1975. The 12-hour bus trip at night from Medellín to Magangué was uneventful. Since our belongings were to arrive the same day we did, we had packed only the clothing we would need for a day or two. Traveling with small children is much easier if you do not have to also lug large suitcases.

Everything we owned was packed in metal barrels and placed on a truck. But as usual, it did not arrive when planned. *Mañana*, the Spanish word for tomorrow, is frequently used in Colombia. The truck with our belongings arrived four days late.

The furniture we would need was to be purchased after we arrived; therefore, we had planned to spend a couple of nights in a hotel allowing time for the purchase and delivery of basic furniture.

The meals served in the hotel were huge. Neither Vernon nor I could eat one meal. So we decided to order two meals and divide them among all the family members. That seemed like a good plan until we discovered it meant we would only receive two glasses of water. Even though there was water all around us, Magangué was in flood season and drinking water was limited. Howard absolutely refused to drink any kind of carbonated beverage. So we saved the water by pouring it into one of our containers. I put halazone tablets in it so I could mix his formula in that water. The rest of us drank carbonated beverages. The girls thought they had reached paradise.

Because everything had been damaged from the flood, the water pressure level was very low in the village. The hotel did not have enough water pressure to provide us with bath water. Therefore, I was not able to give Howard or the girls a bath. Neither could I clean the apartment as the water pressure there would not go up to the third floor.

Vernon was actively seeking solutions to meet our immediate needs. He went into the stores along the business district. A furniture storeowner befriended us. After talking with Vernon, he offered to sell us a two-burner gas stove because he felt we would come through with the money to pay for it. Even though we had some Colombian money, we did not have enough for large purchases. All our money was deposited in bank accounts in the states, so we had to write our checks on those accounts. No one in the village knew us yet. They wisely were not willing to take checks written by strangers on an account in a foreign bank. But that reality did present a problem for us.

Vernon was very thankful for the stove but wondered what good it was if we did not have water available in the apartment. At some point, while he was out and about, he saw a faucet just inside the door at the bottom of the 47 steps. He found a bucket and opened the spigot. Water! So he purchased a hose. The hose was long enough to reach half way up the steps. The pressure was strong enough to get the water only that close to the apartment, but it was much better than having to haul all of the water up from ground-level. Vernon returned to the hotel and said, "Honey, I can get water halfway up the steps, and I have a bucket."

"Okay, we are going," I replied.

I had been thinking, *Water, water everywhere, but not a drop of drinkable water, and no water to bathe the kids.* I responded with a mother's concern, "I have to have someplace to give the kids a bath."

Because we had that little two burner stove, I could boil water. With the boiled water, I could start preparing meals for my family. Besides, we now had access to safe water for drinking and preparing powdered milk for Howard.

With the availability of water, several of my concerns were resolved. I could give the kids a bath. We carried buckets of water up the stairs and gave the children a nice, cold bath by using a gourd dipper to pour water over them. Also, I could start cleaning the apartment. I felt like we were making progress toward transforming that location into our home. Yes, it was a lot of work because we had to carry each bucket of water up the second half of the stairs to the apartment.

Even though the truck had still not arrived with our belongings, we decided to stay in our apartment instead of sleeping in a hotel room. We purchased a junior bed with low sides for Howard. By having the kids lay sideways, all three could sleep on that bed for a few nights. Vernon and I put our ponchos on the tile floor for our bedding. We thought the ponchos would be enough to keep us warm at night. Even though the daytime was hot and humid, the nights did get cold. We slept very little for a couple of nights. But we were content. The facts that we had water to boil for drinking and fixing formula, I could cook a little bit, and we were living in our apartment in the river area were blessings for which we thanked God.

Neighbors, church members, teachers, and storekeepers quickly fell in love with our three white-skinned, blond-haired foreigners. Of course, my kids were not really foreigners since they had lived in Colombia most of their lives.

I set up the one bedroom with the window air conditioner as a homeschool classroom for the two girls. When we moved to Magangué, Colleen was in second grade, and Joyce was in first grade. Howard loved to play in the long corridor just outside the classroom door. He was content to play there for hours while I taught the girls. I held school from 8:00 until 11:30. Our Colombian friends and acquaintances knew that was school time in our home, and they did not visit us until after 11:30.

Our apartment became a drop-off place, a supply room for the schools, an overnight hotel, and a counseling office. The little OMS schools were increasing in number. The opening of new schools meant Vernon began to travel more. Even though that meant more work for us, we were overjoyed. More supplies had to be carried up and down the stairs, more correspondence was necessary, and more planning was required. But the Gospel message was being spread.

Each child who received a scholarship from Compassion International had an individual sponsor. I translated letters sent between children and their sponsors. It was not long until I had two little helpers who could translate from Spanish into English. The girls became quite proficient at translating. I paid them a small amount, like 10 pesos, for a certain number of letters being translated. The girls thought it was great. The girls' help with that responsibility was such a blessing.

Compassion International sponsors gave a set amount of money that was used to pay for school supplies, a school uniform, and most of the tuition for one child. Even if it was only a few pesos, parents had to pay something for the child's education. This way, the parents had an investment in the child's education.

Also, some very basic medical services were provided, as no doctors were available to service most of the rural area. We had to figure out what was needed. Sometimes we provided worm medicine or malaria medicine or something similar. If a child had a severe medical need, funds for treatment costs could be requested. Later on, we were able to provide a good, healthy snack for each child to have in the middle of the morning.

Vernon never came back from his visits to the schools without a list of names of people who needed prayer. The list might have people who had physical needs, who had accepted Christ, or who were in need of salvation. It would include not only those connected with the school, but also community people. He wrote down names of pastors and members of their congregations. People began to greatly appreciate Vernon for his spiritual life. Seeing his lists really spoke to my heart.

He kept the list of names in a little book he always carried with him. Vernon also used that little book to record all of his expenses. Of course, I had record those expenses and keep track of the funds he had not used on each trip as I made my reports to Compassion International. While I performed the bookkeeping responsibilities, I saw the list of names from the most recent trip. When he was home, after breakfast, Vernon would either go into the office or our bedroom to pray for the people on his list. I do not know of a time he prayed for less than an hour over those names.

Praying together in the evening when he was home was a special blessing for me. I put the kids in bed by 7:00 every evening because in those river areas of Colombia, everyone arose around 4:00 a.m. and were out on the streets, making noise. The children could not sleep late because of the village noises. I often said that the Colombians had square-wheeled wheelbarrows because as they went down the sidewalks, the wheels went plump, plump, plump.

In the evenings when Vernon was home, we prayed for local churches, churches along rivers, our schools, the children, and the lost in the village where we were living.

Our dream and our hearts' desire had come true at last. We were living among the Colombian people in the river area.

*****

Millie's insight: God's timing brings joy and brings dreams to fruition.

CHAPTER EIGHTEEN

Smiling at the Storm
Having Faith in God

"The disciples went and woke him, saying, 'Master, Master, we're going to drown!' He got up and rebuked the wind and the raging waters; the storm subsided, and all was calm. 'Where is your faith?' he asked his disciples." Luke 8:24-25a

*****

Millie's insight: Storms may come, but God has a purpose in every cloud. He will guide our vessel if we will let him.

*****

On my first trip into the remote areas of Colombia, I fell in love with the rural Colombian people. Shortly after we were married, Vernon and I took a trip on the river to take the Gospel to the people living along the river. During that trip, which was his first trip into the rural areas, Vernon also lost his heart to the rural people. He would devote the rest of his life taking the Gospel to them. It was a blessing to me that my dear, sweet husband was as heartbroken for the rural Colombians as was I was.

While my blonde-haired daughters were very young, Vernon decided to take them and me on a river trip to visit some of the Christian schools in the remote areas. Colleen was three, and Joyce was two. Both Vernon and I looked forward to the family trip. One of the schools we planned to visit was in Colorado, a village of about 500 people. That location was far back into the interior—so far in fact that one of my friends said the world comes to an end there. Of course that was not true,

127

and eventually I would visit villages farther removed from civilization. But nevertheless, to visit Colorado meant taking a long trip into the rural region. So we made preparations, packed, and boarded a small boat.

Máximo, a Colombian Christian who piloted a boat down these rivers, volunteered to transport us in the mission outboard motor boat on that trip. We headed down the Magdalena River in the tropical heat until we reached smaller bodies of water that led us to our destination. While we were weaving our way back into the interior, our boat pilot had a malaria attack. He was a bit delirious but did his best to navigate the waterways.

Not long after we entered a large swampy area, we knew that we were lost. All we could see was water vegetation. It became impossible to locate the flow of the stream. The men tried unsuccessfully to use poles to steer the boat to a deeper area so the motor would be able to propel us upstream.

It started getting late, and we were making no progress. We were stuck in the middle of a swamp in the middle of a wilderness area. Finally, Vernon and the sick pilot got out of the boat and waded, pushing the boat as they moved toward what they hoped would be the channel.

Lightning started to flash in the clouds. The danger of the lightning striking our boat, or for that matter anything close by, was not my only worry. I knew the waters in the Colombian interior, like the area where my husband and our pilot were wading, held a large population of stingrays, snakes, and alligators. We were lost, the swamp engulfed us, night was fast approaching, and a storm was building up not far from our location. I prayed for God's protection.

Time passed, and we still were stuck in the middle of the swamp. I was becoming not only concerned for the men but also anxious for those two precious blonde-headed preschool girls. Much to my surprise, the girls suddenly burst out singing a praise hymn. "With Christ in the vessel, we can smile at the storm and drive the clouds away."[2] They apparently believed if they sang to God, the storm clouds with the threatening lightning would stay far away from them. The girls thought it was great fun singing at the clouds. What an experience to see those two small girls singing in Spanish with great gusto.

Our young daughters exhibited more faith than we did. What were we to fear? I wondered why I had been so worried. Yes, it was true that we could see no people and no vessels. No one was coming to our rescue. All we could see was the swamp surrounding us. But God was watching over us.

The two-year-old was quite charming at times and throughout the day had provided some relief to our spirits with her comments. She had apparently developed affection for our pilot during our ordeal. She called our guide, "*mi* (my) Máximo."

Darkness was falling quickly. Suddenly, I saw a light flickering in the distance and pointed it out to the men. The men climbed into the boat. They could not use the paddles to propel the boat, as the vegetation was too thick and there was not enough water to help them get through it. Máximo was very sick, and Vernon was almost at the end of his strength. Instead of the paddles, they had to use the long poles to laboriously move toward that distant light.

Finally, we could discern the outline of a small island in the middle of the swamp. After the men pulled the boat on the shore, we learned one family lived on that small island. Vernon asked if we could tie up the boat and hang our hammocks in the trees for the night. To our dismay, the family told us to move on up the swamp. I understood their reluctance because we were total strangers. The island family had no way of knowing if we meant them harm. Maybe others traveling in the swamp had treated that family poorly or maybe they had heard stories of people mistreating a small group such as them. It made no difference what the reason was; they did not want us to stay there.

Before we left, the head of the family, in true Colombian style, pointed his chin in the direction we should go. Our exhausted group reluctantly boarded the boat and proceeded in that direction. Vernon and I were sad because we had not been given a chance to rest nor to witness to that poor family. Our only option was to push our boat back into the swamp.

Before long, Máximo was able to locate the stream right where the man had pointed with his chin. But by that time,

Máximo had a high fever and was totally exhausted. His body gave out, and he crumpled over. Not only did Vernon and I have two preschool girls to care for and protect, but now we also had a sick and incapacitated guide.

I was just being practical when I suggested to Vernon that we pull the boat up to shore and tie it to a tree. The hammocks could be placed on the bottom of the boat, and we could cover over with the mosquito netting. Besides, it was much too dangerous to continue. The wildlife and alligators were especially dangerous on those small streams at night. The possibility of hitting a rock or debris in the dark and damaging or overturning the boat was a real threat. Besides, we all needed some sleep.

Máximo had recovered a bit of strength but still was barely able to help land the boat. Vernon was tying the boat to a tree when the little ones became frightened, as did each person in our traveling group. We heard the deep, vicious barking of dogs. It was evident that the dogs would be on us in just moments. The suddenness of the dogs' appearance and the knowledge that dogs often could be quite vicious in defending their territory from intruders, especially unannounced night intruders, made the barking terrifying. Dogs also meant that people were close by. Would they be violent, tolerate us, send us back into the swamp, or be friendly? We would soon find out.

Flashlights started to come toward us from somewhere inland. Three men approached. Máximo explained who we were and where we were going. He also explained that we were exhausted and could not go any farther. He asked for permission to tie up the boat and to set up our hammocks for the night.

As soon as Máximo told the men with the flashlights that we were evangelical Christians, the three men enthusiastically welcomed us. What a relief. The men helped secure the boat and removed the outboard motor so it could be stored in a safer location. They did not want it to be stolen. These strangers then warmly invited us into their home.

The settlement consisted of one extended family that all lived in one small house. This family had been evangelized many years before when an OMS missionary had traveled in a remote area where they were living at that time. Even though that day's travels and trials had left us exhausted, we had quite a time of Bible study and prayer, using candlelight and flashlights. Our exhaustion was tempered by the joy and pleasure of sharing time and faith with each other.

One of the little girls in the family had whooping cough. She coughed constantly the whole evening. The family had been unable to do anything for that precious little girl other than to give her some herbs. Medical help was not available in that remote region. The little girl had dutifully stayed in an area by herself away from us. Her coughing caught Vernon's attention. It broke his heart to know how miserable she must be. After we had completed the prayer service, Vernon asked the little girl to come to him. Vernon and I prayed with the family over that precious little one. Her coughing stopped. The next morning she was happily running around, playing with her family and visiting with her new friends. It was a beautiful example of God's healing touch.

After the worship service, hammocks were unpacked and places to hang them were found. My hammock was hung over the table. Colleen, my oldest daughter, slept with me. Joyce was quite proud of her new little hammock and was glad she would finally get to use it. Her hammock was hung close to me. Máximo just laid his hammock on the table under Colleen and me. Vernon's hammock was hung in the lean-to kitchen, which was just poles covered with a thatched roof. Mosquito netting was unfurled. I had no idea where the family who had given us shelter holed up for the night—probably some slept outside in hammocks and some slept in the other little room where there must have been a bed or place for some of them to sleep. I do know that I was glad for a safe place to rest. The hospitality of this precious family was endearing.

However, during the night I heard scratching sounds. I was deathly afraid of rats and did not want them around my dear, beloved daughter in the hammock by herself. Every time I heard scratching, I would reach out to shake her hammock, hoping to scare the rats away. Joyce had a nice swaying sleep that night. The next morning, relief swept over me, and I had a good laugh, when I learned the nighttime sounds had come from a mother cat scratching her claws on the rope.

After we awoke, we quickly took down the hammocks and removed our things from the family's living space. My daughters disappeared in the hustle and bustle of early morning activities. I was a bit anxious, wondering where the girls could have wandered to and what danger they could get themselves into in this location. What a relief when I found them watching one of the men milking the cow. My daughters laughed and squealed as the man squirted the warm milk directly into their wide-open mouths. I am sure that was the beginning of Colleen's love for fresh unpasteurized milk.

Vernon and I joyfully spent the morning teaching the Bible to that dear family. They so much wanted to learn more about the Lord. Their hearts and minds were open to everything they learned from us. I felt like royalty. This precious family gave us their best hospitality and were so grateful for the teaching we provided. For me, all the trials of the trip were neutralized by the joy I experienced as I developed a relationship with this small group of Christians. It was hard to leave, but people in other villages were expecting us.

The family asked us to return. Vernon said we would if we had the opportunity. However, we never did encounter that family again as we could not find the location. We knew it was in the state of Bolivar in the northwestern region of Colombia. We even traveled several times back to the village where we were going when we had the chance meeting with this family. God had truly ordained that special visit and richly blessed the encounter. The Lord had led us to that secret place to find the hidden treasures he had established. God had placed our family in the swampy wilderness to encourage that dear family. And that dear family blessed us—lost travelers. They were a hidden Colombian treasure.

*****

Millie's insight: With Christ's presence, storm clouds turn into beautiful refreshing joy.

CHAPTER NINETEEN

Sowing With Tears

"Those who sow with tears will reap with songs of joy. Those who go out weeping, carrying seed to sow, will return with songs of joy, carrying sheaves with them." Psalm 126:5–6

*****

Millie's insight: We sow, and God gives the harvest if the seeds are watered with our tears.

*****

In 1974, when Vernon and I left Medellín to distribute Christmas gifts and school supplies to 10 of the Christian schools along the river area. At that time we had a nine-month-old, a six-year-old, and a seven-year-old. We left our children at the Peniel Bible Institute under the care of two single missionary women. I must admit that Vernon and I were quite a show as we headed to the bank of the river with our boxes and suitcases.

That year, the rivers were extremely swollen because the annual floods were unusually high. Little was left of livestock and crops along the river regions. Fields were flooded and drowned animals were floating down the waterways. No food was available, and dry places to sleep were almost nonexistent. Conditions were incredibly bad.

We went into one little school after another and waited to see the children who came to us. Some of the children were already quite sick because of the severe conditions. But they came because it was so important to them to receive a small Christmas gift, register for school, get a school uniform, and receive their school supplies for the next school term, which would start after the summer break.

During that trip, I watched the children come to us day after day. No matter where we were, the children generally came in dugout canoes and on stilts. Sometimes, because it was impossible to see through the muddy floodwater, a stilt would suddenly hit a hole or a low place under the water. The child would tumble into the water and emerge laughing as if it was a fun game they were playing. Other children met us wrapped in towels or in whatever cloth item they could find that was dry. As I looked at those children, I wandered how many of them would survive the epidemic illnesses caused by the flooded, unsanitary conditions in which they had to live. Medical care was primitive or nonexistent as hospitals and doctors were not available in the remote regions. I wondered how many of the children would be alive and well enough to enter the schoolroom in a couple of months when classes began again after the school break.

One day, it was especially sad, or maybe it was the cumulative effect of seeing the deplorable situations day after day. I started weeping as we pulled away from the village we had been visiting. Before long, I lost it. I began crying uncontrollably as we traveled down that flood-swollen river. Vernon reached over to comfort me and said, "Honey, it will only be a few more days, and we will be back with the kiddies." He thought I was missing our children, and I was. But that was not the reason for my uncontrollable crying that day.

My heart was broken for those children living in the awful conditions up and down the river that summer. Those children could have been ours. Why had we been so privileged? Our children had so much more than the little ones we had been seeing. I was glad our children were blessed, but it seemed unfair. I kept asking myself what I could do to help.

I remember crying out that day, "Oh God, give me many, many spiritual children from these rural areas, from the cities, throughout this country. Give me sons and daughters out here for your kingdom." I thought of Hannah crying out for a son in

1 Samuel 1:11. And God gave her a son. As I prayed for spiritual sons and daughters among the Colombians, I asked God for those that would give their lives to serve him.

That night our boat pulled up to a little thatched hut with bamboo walls. We had to jump to a platform to keep our feet out of the water. The people living in that hut had hung hammocks just under the thatch roof to have a dry place to sleep. What few belongings they had were also stored just under the roof to protect them from floodwaters. This was the normal living condition for people in the river areas that year. Even though it was a difficult trip, God brought in a harvest from the seeds that were sown.

Some of those children gave their lives to teaching others about salvation found in Jesus. I remember a dedicated graduate from our Bible institute who gave her life to the education of the children in one of these remote areas. She carried her seed out and planted. And yes, God gave a harvest.

Her son was just two years old when she started teaching. Wilmer finished fifth grade under the instruction of his mom in that river village. Then he had the privilege of going to our Christian dorm in Magangué. For six years, he attended our Christian high school there. During those years, he rapidly grew in the Lord, he helped in the local church, and he evangelized in nearby villages. In his teen years, he became a supply pastor for his hometown church during the summer vacation months. After he graduated from high school, he returned to his hometown to serve as pastor. Wilmer continues in pastoral work. He is not unique. This pattern has been repeated over and over with the fruit harvested at our Christian dorm and school whose students were gleaned from the many little Christian primary schools in the rural areas.

We spread God's Word in many locations. It took years as we sowed seeds among the hardened men involved in the drug cartels, guerilla activities, and police corruption who were all imprisoned in Bellavista Prison in Medellín. In the 1970s and 1980s, this prison was reputed to be the most violent prison in Colombia as well as one of the most violent prisons in the whole world.

If you could have witnessed the scene I did during one of my first visits to the prison, you would have leaped for joy. The majority of the 250 prisoners who gathered in the chapel built by OMS within the prison walls were young men between the ages of 16 and 30. Most had scars from wounds that should have resulted in their deaths, but God had spared them. That morning, 30 of those prisoners entered into baptismal waters right there in the prison chapel. They held hands and lifted them high in praise to God. As they worshiped God in that little chapel, their faces shone. While watching them, I thought of Moses' face as it was described in Exodus 34:29. God was alive in them. There had been weeping, sowing, and now leaping for joy. For most of them, this was the result of seed that had been watered over and over again with prayer.

Many of those incarcerated men had young children at home, and they wanted their children to learn about God's love. Once a month children were allowed to visit their fathers on the patio in the prison. I had the joy of giving seminars, instructing them how to present the Gospel to their children. I taught them how to present the salvation story using the flannel board, puppets, children's songs, and Bible verses. I taught them not only how to use the materials, but also how to lead their children to Christ. All around the patio area on visitation day, those men could be seen presenting Gospel stories to their children.

A lot of those prisoners who have completed their sentences and have been released from jail are serving God with their lives. A surprising number of them have gone through seminary. Some have started feeding programs for children on the streets. It is amazing what these "hopeless criminals" have done once they accepted Jesus as their Savior.

As God's servants we go out carrying our little bag of seed and sowing. What a blessing it is to see the harvest. We return with songs of joy bringing in the sheaves.

*****

Millie's insight: It will take years as we sow to bring in precious treasures from those hidden places.

CHAPTER TWENTY

Wading Through the Waters

"When you pass through the waters, I will be with you;
and when you pass through the rivers, they will not sweep
over you. When you walk through the fire, you will not be
burned; the flames will not set you ablaze. For I am the LORD,
your God, the Holy One of Israel, your Savior."
Isaiah 43:2–3a

*****

Millie's insight: The rivers may overflow, the nights are dark,
and the storms are fierce, but God will be with us and bring us
through to victory. He often carries us through when we would
faint—all because he loves us so.

*****

The year of 1975 was an outstanding year for our work for the
Lord. Vernon traveled to established schools and new schools
that he had founded. These trips were often into remote areas.
Many of our Colombian national friends said Vernon had gone
into areas they would tremble to enter. As long as there were
children who needed an education and lost souls to be saved,
Vernon was willing to trek into those areas. No place was too
remote as long as God was calling him to go. We were encouraged, and we praised God.

137

The rainy season began as usual toward the end of October. During a normal year, the smaller rivers flooded at least once. Naturally, we were hoping it would not flood in our area like it had the year before nor like a few years earlier when we had taken our first trip down the river together.

But as November approached, the waters began to rise more and more as a result of the plentiful rains. Before long, the waters were over the riverbanks. In Magangué, it appeared that the water would not stop rising for some time. We were sad because this terrible flooding would mean another year of lost crops, animals dying, and disease. We knew we would see people in the rural areas without food and with flooded homes. Sadly, the government gave very little help to the flooded rural areas. Eventually, we were able to get some help from Compassion International to take food into many of the regions where the destruction was extremely acute. Vernon would fill a little outboard motor boat with whatever supplies we could acquire for the people. He then traveled up and down the rivers to make deliveries to those in need.

Sadly, no doctors were available to treat people afflicted with disease caused by unsanitary conditions that were a direct result of the floodwaters. As far as medical help was concerned, we could do very little.

The streets in Magangué actually became rivers. People traveled through the streets in outboard motor boats and dugout canoes. One thing we did not have to worry about was water getting into our apartment because we lived on the third floor. During this flooding, I became very thankful that we had those 47 stairs to climb.

However, the prevalent rats were very smart creatures, so when the water, rose they moved to higher areas. I did not like the idea that rats were moving closer to my apartment in search of food. Soon they would be raiding the garbage that I had been collecting. Because of the flood conditions, no garbage collection was available. As far as I was concerned, those rats should be kept as far as possible from my small children. Before long, it became evident that the garbage would have to be removed from the apartment if we were going to avoid a rat infestation in our home. What was I to do? It was a mystery. There was no place to take the garage. Water was everywhere.

Finally we put all of our garbage into black bags. Vernon took them two at a time down the stairs to the street. As he stood waist deep in water, in desperation, he looked around then turned loose of the bags. From the third-story balcony, I watched those bags rapidly float down the Magdalena River. Many times, Vernon had told the children that they could not throw things out of the window of a car, even if it was only a seed. Even though we had seen many others throw their refuse in the street and into the floodwaters, we hated having to do it ourselves. But there were only two options: turn it loose on the floodwaters or have a rat-infested home.

Just a few minutes later, I heard our doorbell ring. I went to the balcony to see who was visiting at such a time. It was Vernon. He called up, "Honey, from that box of tracts in the office, bring me a packet of the ones titled '*El Gran Diluvio*'" ("The Great Flood"). The English translation is "The Great Flood." I quickly took the tracts to the ground-level door. Then Vernon stood in the middle of the street for some time. When canoes and motorboats traveled down the street, he gave out those tracts. He had recognized the flooded streets as an opportunity to share the Good News about God's love and provision. It was an effective method of witnessing to many people that would be inaccessible otherwise.

The children could not get out of the house to play. The floodwaters were much too dangerous. One of their pastimes during that flood was standing on our-third floor balcony watching the people pass by. They especially enjoyed an area where the city had started paving the street toward the building where we lived. Because of the rains, the roadwork had stopped almost by our building. Where they stopped the road construction, there was a large drop-off that was hidden by the muddy floodwater.

The children watched people wade down the street. As people approached the hidden drop-off, the kids would start saying, "They're going to fall. They're going to fall. They fell!" Then they squealed and laughed. It was a game for the children, as it seemed to be for the local people who would pick themselves up and laugh. They apparently viewed traveling the streets with the unseen holes as an adventure full of surprises for them. Most Americans would not have found humor in the situation, but maybe that is because in the United States we do not live through yearly severe flood conditions.

After school the children would watch people fall into the floodwaters until it was dark. After dark, when the people and boats were no longer moving down the street, they enjoyed watching the flooded street for an entirely different reason. Snakes. Without people stirring up the mud, the water became clear enough to see the myriad of snakes. The children loved watching them, but I cringed. I knew those snakes were there in the daytime when Vernon or I had to venture out. I did not ask if they were poisonous. All I knew was that my boots only came to my knees and the water was up to my hips. I feared that one of those creepy creatures would get into one of my boots.

The floods lasted for weeks, and everyone had to go about taking care of daily necessities. Businesses made adjustments and continued serving their customers. Banking during the flood was a unique experience. The river had invaded our bank as water flowed right through it. The bank accommodated its customers by building some wooden steps to the counter where people did their banking business. The bank employees used electric typewriters to record business transactions. The typewriters were plugged into cords hanging temporarily from the ceiling. All I could think was that I was glad I was not working there because it looked like a dangerous arrangement for those bank employees. They were standing in the flowing water and using electricity at the same time.

The local post office kept its doors open longer than it should have. I remember seeing letters floating on top of the water as they went out of sight. A bank across the street from the post office was built high enough so water was not flowing through it. The post office moved all the mail to that bank. All around the edges of the bank, the mail was laid on the floor. I thought as I went in to get my mail that it would be in alphabetical order. No way. Letters had been laid around the room

140

in random order. To get my mail, I had to go through all of the mail that was scattered about. I am sure we missed mail, but fortunately nothing of importance, as far as I know.

Shopping was another challenge. I didn't have room to stock a big supply of food, so regular trips to the market were necessary. I needed to purchase vegetables and meat at least once a week, if not more often. During the flood, I took our maid with me to market because it took the two of us to hold each other down in the areas with more swiftly moving water. The market was about a 10-block trek from the apartment.

I especially remember one time going to church during the floods while Vernon was on a trip. All three of my energetic children were finally ready to go to church. The girls and I donned our boots, I picked up Howard, and off we went through the waters. The floodwaters were low enough that the girls could walk with me. However, by the time we arrived at church, all of us were wet. We took off our boots and went barefoot into the church. The only thing we could do was to sit there and worship even though we were very damp. Other worshipers were just as wet as we were.

After the floodwaters had been invading our street for some time, Vernon knew the kids needed to get out of the house to play. They had been cooped up in those four walls for weeks. So one afternoon, he decided to treat them to a few minutes of fun. He took them out in their little swimming suits to play in the water. The next day, all three children had fevers. Vernon felt so bad. That was the last time they went out to play in the floodwater.

Around Thanksgiving time, two fellows came down from Men for Missions (a ministry of OMS). John and Herb Schultz were to make shelves for our office, as well as for the kitchen, as I had no kitchen cabinets. Toward the end of their stay, Vernon wanted to take them to visit one of our schools that was not too far from us.

To make this trip, they needed new shoes because their shoes, which were adequate for the planned activities, were not satisfactory for going into the rural area. We were sure we could not find boots for them so we settled on helping them shop for tennis

141

shoes. Only two stores in Magangué sold shoes. John and Herb tried on shoes and tried on shoes. The clerks laughed and laughed at the men as they shopped for shoes. And anybody who happened to enter the store stood laughing at them. Their feet were hilariously big by Colombian standards. Luckily, John and Herb had a good sense of humor and finally found shoes they could wear without squeezing their feet too tightly.

At the end of their stay, Vernon traveled with those two men on the bus as far as Barranquilla. Vernon needed to stay in Barranquilla overnight because he could not catch a returning bus until the next day. That night, the Lord spoke to him about his father's health. Because of this new concern for his father, Vernon called his sister Joyce before he left Barranquilla. She told him that their father had been low physically for a while and was currently in the hospital. His father had been diagnosed with cancer. The hope was that the doctor could operate and remove it. Vernon prayed for his father's health, for his mother, and for his family during this time of illness.

The Colombian tradition is to have a large celebration on Christmas Eve. Christmas Day celebrations are of secondary importance. Colombians serve a big meal at midnight on Christmas Eve. Quite often, the Christian churches have a Christmas Eve program, which goes until midnight.

That year, I stayed at home because Howard had not been feeling well. Vernon took the two girls to the Christmas Eve program. Just as I was finishing Howard's bath, the doorbell rang. I quickly wrapped him in a towel and carried him as I ran down the steps. It was Camilo's errand boy. He was delivering a gift from his boss to us.

As I went back up the steps, I thought the package felt like it held a bottle of liquor. I put it on the shelf in the office. After Vernon was home and the girls were in bed, I told him that Camilo had sent a gift. The next morning Vernon opened the package. It was an expensive imported bottle of liquor. Vernon told me, "I don't know what to do exactly." He decided to not make an immediate decision.

The day after Christmas, Vernon went into the office to pray as he did most days when he was home. When he came out, he said, "There are three things I can do. I can open the bottle and pour it down the drain. I can give it to someone else. Or I can return it to Camilo. I don't want to offend him. So will you pray with me?"

After a time of prayer, Vernon looked at me and said, "I'm going to give it back. I'll explain to Camilo that I do not drink and that I appreciate the gift. I will tell him I did not want to throw it away and have him think that I had drunk it. Nor do I want to give it to someone else and be a part of his drinking habit. I will express my appreciation for the gift and that I hope he understands."

Camilo accepted Vernon's returned gift and explanation. About a week later, the errand boy came back to our house with another gift. It was a beautiful black and gold vase, which probably was imported. I carried it home in my hands when I returned to the United States in 2003, as I feared it might get broken if it traveled in the other luggage. Camilo told Vernon that he respected us because we were absolutely honest about our relationship with God.

Early in January, when he had access to telephone service, Vernon called Joyce again. They were very close as she was almost like a mother to him. His mother had been very sick when he was young, and it was Joyce who had cared for him. During that call, he learned that the cancer had spread throughout his father's body. His father had decided to live the remainder of his life at home with his family around him. During this call, Joyce told Vernon that if he wanted to see his father while he was still alive, he should return home as soon as possible.

Floodwaters were still a problem, so Vernon traipsed through the water with a traveling suitcase. He secured a canoe to travel to the bus station. He traveled by bus to Medellín, hoping to quickly get the required written permit to re-enter Colombia. At that time, he would have been denied reentry into Colombia if he did not have the required written permit. For some reason, there was a delay at the official offices in issuing the permit.

Vernon's father died before he arrived in Wisconsin. But

143

Vernon felt it was a blessing that he had arrived in time for the funeral.

OMS always tried to have a representative from the home office or the regional director attend funerals of relatives of OMS missionaries. Vernon and I had worked closely with Bob and Lois Tabor, the regional directors in Iowa at that time. They were designated as the representatives of OMS to attend the funeral. As Bob was leaving to return to Iowa after the funeral, Vernon stopped him in the back of the church. He said, "Bob, I'd like to ask you to pray with me. I just feel our time is so short in Colombia, and there is so much to be done." Little did we know how short.

Meanwhile, the children and I traveled to Medellín to attend the OMS annual missionary meeting. When Vernon returned to Colombia, he met us there for the meetings. It was wonderful to have Vernon with us again.

*****

Millie's insight: I can say it no better than these words written by the songwriter Anna L. Coghill:

> "Work, for the night is coming,
> Under the sunset skies.
> While the bright tints are glowing,
> Work, for daylight flies.
> Work till the last beam fadeth,
> Fadeth to shine no more.
> Work while the night is dark'ning,
> When man's work is o'er."[3]

CHAPTER TWENTY-ONE

Time Is Short

"But I trust in you, O LORD; I say, 'You are my God.'
My times are in your hands." Psalm 31:14-15a

*****

Millie's insight: Let's work while there is time to work.

*****

Vernon met the children and me in Medellín when he returned to Colombia after his father's funeral. We had traveled there for the annual OMS Colombia missionary meetings. We looked forward to those annual meetings, as it was a time to be with friends we seldom saw. It was such a joy to hear all that had been accomplished during the previous year, discuss how to achieve those goals that were not completed, and plan for the new year of ministry. The meetings were an encouraging challenge to each of us to press forward.

When the meetings ended, Vernon left for the state of Santander del Sur on January 25 with great excitement for what God had for us for 1976. He would visit the two schools that were the farthest from our home in Magangué. To travel to the first school from our home would take Vernon 2½ days. The second school required another 1½ days' travel time. To reach these remote schools, Vernon would travel by bus, train, boat, mule, and on foot. He figured he would be gone at least two weeks. This meant that he would return home around February 15.

Vernon left for his trip during the afternoon; the children and I left that same evening on the 12-hour bus ride back to Magangué.

On Monday morning, February 9, the children and I began talking about what we were going to do in preparation for Daddy's return. Each time Vernon returned home from an extended trip, the children did something special to welcome him home. They made little announcements, along with "Welcome Home Daddy" and "We are happy to have you back" signs. Sometimes they were in Spanish, and sometimes they were in English.

It was a few minutes before 8:00 in the morning on February 9. As usual, I was setting things up in the bedroom for the girls' school. The phone rang. It was quite startling as that was the first time the phone had rung in almost three months. During and following the flood season, especially one as bad as it had been that year, the phones didn't work, so I was a bit surprised to hear ours ring. I was also a bit excited, as normal communication was returning after the floods.

The reception was not very good. All I understood at the time was the call was from Medellín. This, too, was puzzling because the telephone office in Magangué normally was not open before eight o'clock. I was cut off before I could even learn whom the caller was. Just as I was returning to the bedroom, the phone rang again. This time the clear voice of Florence Cavender, secretary to Bruce Hess the OMS Colombia field leader, was on the other end of the line. Florence's first comment was that Bruce and his wife Donna were on their way to catch a Missionary Aviation Fellowship (MAF) plane. I was trying to figure out why she was telling me this. My lack of response made her pause for a moment. Then she said, "Millie, have you heard anything?"

I responded, "No. About Vernon?"

"Yes. Vernon was in an accident on his way into Plan de Armas." And again Florence paused.

The fact that Vernon had been hurt and I needed to get to him was running through my mind.

OMS missionaries often called adults aunts and uncles, making us more like family to each other. She said, "Aunt Millie,

146

he is with the Lord." Immediately we lost contact. No more information. I was stunned by her message.

I took my three small children on my lap with my arms wrapped around them. I told them Daddy was with Jesus and Grandpa Young. Colleen immediately said, "Mommy, who is going to visit the little schools now? You cannot do that, teach us, and do the office work." She was only eight, but she understood the importance of the work her father was doing for the Lord.

When I returned to Magangué after the annual OMS missionary meetings in Medellín, I had brought with me a young teenager to help with office work, a teacher who was waiting to go into a river village to teach, and a woman who was going to sew school uniforms for area children. I sent one of the girls, I honestly do not remember which one, to the local OMS church to let them know.

People soon started hearing of Vernon's tragedy and came to the house. A Colombian custom is to serve coffee to people who come to mourn and comfort the family. A member of the family did not usually do it. However, all of our friends were in such shock that no one was performing the social function, so I did it. Having that responsibility, in addition to taking care of my children's needs, was probably good for me as we waited and waited and waited for more information.

The MAF plane bringing Bruce and Donna didn't arrive at the small airport in Magangué until 1:00 p.m. I was surprised to know that MAF was in Colombia. I later learned that only about a month earlier, Bruce had met Jim Hurd, the MAF pilot, by chance at the Medellín airport. MAF had only been in Colombia for about two months. God had brought them just in time for my need.

We left on the plane around 2:00 p.m. Our pilot, Bruce and Donna Hess, my children, and I filled that little plane to its capacity. I held Howard in my lap while the girls had to sit in the back of the plane, which was generally used for baggage. Colleen had never liked flying, and this was her first time in a little airplane. As we were getting ready to take off, I noticed she was as stiff as a board. She was scared to death. To reassure her, I put one hand back so both she and Joyce could hold it.

147

During much of that flight, I held Howard in one hand and extended my other hand backwards to comfort the girls.

Shortly after we were in the air, someone started singing the song "God Is So Good." We sang that little song over and over, singing about every verse that was possible. Eventually, the girls, who were just eight and six, became exhausted from all that was happening and fell asleep. Howard, since he was 1½ years old, understood very little of what was happening. But he knew something different was taking place.

At that point, we knew very little of what had happened. While I was still at home, I had received several phone calls. Based on information we received from those phone calls, we believed that Vernon's body had been taken to Cimitarra, where an air force base was located. Small civilian aircrafts were prohibited from flying in the region because it was a military airport. However, Jim was able to get permission to land there.

We would arrive around 4:00 p.m. Jim realized that would not work because we could not land, unload, find out what had happened, and get out of there in time to arrive at Medellín before 6:00 p.m., the time that the airport closed. So, in mid-air we changed course. We landed at Puerto Berrio.

The decision was made that Jim would fly the three children and Donna back to Medellín, where Donna would care for them. Bruce and I would stay in Puerto Berrio until we could learn the location of Vernon's body and make arrangements to have it taken to Medellín. Before the airplane took off, Colleen said, "Mommy, I will see you in the morning." My heart was heavy for my daughter as I watched the plane taxi to the runway with her little face pressed to the window. I thought, *What a trauma for an eight-year-old!*

The airport was about four miles from Puerto Berrio. I couldn't believe that there were no telephones at the airport nor any taxis to transport people into town. We sent a boy to a neighbor down the road to try to call for a taxi to pick us up and take us into Puerto Berrio. We waited and waited.

During that time of waiting, Bruce asked me if Vernon ever mentioned anything about anyone threatening him. I answered, "No. Vernon had nothing but good words about people all along the way, both the believers and the nonbelievers. Why did you ask me that?" I was a bit startled by the question.

Apparently there had been an article in a Bogotá newspaper about Vernon's death. The way it was written made it sound as if there was a question as to whether his death was an accident or the result of some criminal activity.

I went into the restroom and said aloud, "Lord, if this has been purposely done, do not hold this sin against that person." That comes from what Stephen said as he was being stoned for his faith in Acts 7:16.

Finally, we started walking, but before we had gone far, the taxi arrived. Since we had been unable to make definite contact with the officials, we went to the areas in Puerto Berrio where we thought we might get some information. But we learned nothing. So we contacted another taxi driver who said he would take us to Cimitarra, which was a two-hour overland trip. It had been a long traumatic day, I still had few details about Vernon's death, and I still did not know for sure where his body was.

We didn't arrive in Cimitarra until 9:00 p.m. The first place we went was the police office. The police told us Vernon's body was in the evangelical church. They took us over to another place where some of the city officials were having a party. We didn't get much cooperation from them. We were told that we would not be able to take the body out that night nor could we take it out over land, but they might give us permission to take it out by plane the next day. Finally, we had found Vernon's body and knew whom we had to deal with to get it transported to Medellín.

Right after we finished talking with the police, three believers from Plan de Armas and the pastor of Cimitarra showed up. We learned from them more of the details of what happened. Because we did not know what else to do, we went to the church. We were a bit numb from the events of that day, and we needed a place to pray and figure out what to do next.

Two believers from Plan de Armas had left on foot on Saturday morning to seek help to get Vernon's body out. It took them eight hours traveling by foot before they could reach the road to take a bus to Cimitarra. They contacted the oil company for help. The oil company was willing to use their helicopter to airlift the body out, so the men flew in to Plan de Armas with

149

the helicopter pilot. In the meantime, the believers in Plan de Armas had made a wooden coffin and placed Vernon's body in it. When the helicopter arrived with the two men, the body was ready to be transported.

The coffin was attached to one of the helicopter rails. To balance the load, one of the men rode on the other rail as the helicopter traveled over the mountains. This dear man admitted that several times his breath had been taken away as they flew over the rugged terrain. He had risked his life to make it possible for Vernon's body to be returned to me. That was a true display of Christian love for Vernon and the work he was doing in their village.

By the time we reached the church, believers were already waiting for us. We had a time of prayer and Scripture reading. Bruce talked with that dear group of believers about our desire to fly Vernon's body back to Medellín for burial, the need to take care of the paperwork, and the necessity to gain permission to take Vernon's body. Since it was too late in the evening to make any contacts for transporting the body to Medellín, we decided it was best to get a little rest and begin early the next morning.

Before leaving the church that evening, Bruce suggested that in order to expedite the process, we should divide into three groups. The local pastor's group would go immediately in the morning to get a coffin, as the coffin used to bring Vernon out of the jungle would not close anymore. Another group would go to the military base and to the oil company to get a plane to transport the coffin and us out. The pastor from Plan de Armas and I would go to the official offices to get the death certificate, claim the items found on his body, and secure the permit to transport him by plane to Medellín.

Thankfully, those dear believers in Cimitarra made arrangements for Bruce and me to stay in two different homes so we could attempt to get a little sleep.

Cimitarra had two funeral homes, but neither had a ready-made coffin. So they contacted a man and convinced him to drop his plans for the day. He took measurements and made an adequate coffin.

Bruce thought they had made a contact and would be able to get a plane out of Bucarranga. However, with February fogs

150

and the size of plane needed for transporting the coffin, we endured delay after delay. One plane was not big enough. Another plane couldn't land where we were. Another could not get out of where they were because of the fog. It was just one thing after another.

We decided to go back into town around noon and eat lunch. Just as we were ready to go into a restaurant, someone brought the news that the plane we had made arrangements for was almost ready to land. So, of course we immediately went to the airport.

I will never forget those believers from Cimitarra and those three dear men from Plan de Armas staying right by my side through the whole thing. When I realized the men from Plan de Armas had only one bus available that day which could take them to a stop-off point from which they could walk to their homes, I suggested they go catch the bus. I thanked them for all their help and assured them things were settled for our trip to Medellín. The pastor looked at me and said, "Doña Mildred, we will stay by you until the plane flies out of sight." They may not have been blood and flesh relatives, but I am telling you, they were people with warm hearts.

*****

Millie's insight: When we belong to the family of God, we are not alone. I thought of that chorus "The Family of God," written by Bill and Gaither, which says,

"I'm so glad I'm a part of the family of God.
I've been washed in the fountain, cleansed by his blood!
Joint heirs with Jesus as we travel this sod.
For I'm a part of the family, the family of God."[4]

Although no blood family was by my side, my wonderful family of God in Colombia was ever present to love, comfort, and support me.

CHAPTER TWENTY-TWO

Saying Goodbye

"The mighty man will become tinder and his work a spark;
both will burn together, with no one to quench the fire."
Isaiah 1:31

*****

Millie's insight: In times of hurt, one realizes the myriad of friends
who have been influenced by a faithful, genuine Christian servant.
These friends carry us through the valley.

*****

It had been a long day and a half since I learned that Vernon
had passed from this life. The difficulties and trials would have
been unbearable without assistance and guidance from a dedicated and precious group of believers—the men who were
helping me with details and the dear friends who were caring
for my young children.

We finally flew out of Cimitarra a little after one. My mind
was racing, and I was filled with grief. I knew a funeral
service would take place, and I assumed it would be a simple
service, for we would need to have Vernon buried before the
cemetery closed for the evening at 5:30. I was confident that
someone at the OMS compound would have made the necessary arrangements for the cemetery plot. However, my thoughts
were mostly about my children. I missed them and longed to
hold them close to me.

We arrived at the Medellín airport at 2:15. A funeral car was
waiting. I remember being asked if I wanted the body to be

taken to the funeral home so Vernon could be placed in another casket. I knew it would be easier for me, and especially for the children, if Vernon was placed in a nice casket instead of that rough-hewn coffin. But I did not know if there was time to make the change because we had arrived so late. I was concerned because I knew people were waiting at the church for the funeral. I wondered if it would even be possible to transfer him from that rough coffin to a nice casket because of the condition of his body. The funeral director told me it could be done, and it would not take very long to make that arrangement. So they took the body to the funeral home for the change in coffins.

When I arrived at the church, I went in the back way to freshen myself a bit and to take an aspirin. The past few hours had been unbelievably trying. I was physically exhausted and emotionally drained. I then walked out into the sanctuary and saw my daughters coming toward me. My two precious, little girls were wearing darling new dresses.

I will never forget the thoughtfulness of my missionary friends. Even though I had quickly thrown a change of clothes for the children into a suitcase before we left Magangué, they were not the type of clothing to wear to a funeral. Donna Hess had lovingly accompanied the children in that little plane to Medellín, and Phyllis Brown Gutierrez then took over for her after they landed. My dear friend, Phyllis took the girls to the store and bought each of them a nice little dress and then made purses to carry over their arms. They looked so precious at their father's funeral. I, however, had on the same white dress I had put on the morning before. I had worn it on planes and over dusty roads, and I had slept fitfully in that dress. I had no chance to change. So it was especially meaningful to know someone had taken such loving and thoughtful care of my children.

As soon as she reached me, Colleen asked, "Mommy, why are all of the flowers here? Who brought them?" She had not attended a funeral before.

I gently explained, "Honey, the people who loved your daddy and those who are here for the funeral brought them."

She said, "Oh, there are a lot of people who loved Daddy."

154

The funeral service began at 3:45. In spite of the fact we had to be finished at the cemetery before 5:30 when the gates closed, the service kept going on and on. It seemed that everyone wanted to recognize how Vernon had served his God.

All of the officials who had worked with Vernon participated: the former president of the national church association, the current president of the national church association, the coordinator of Every Community for Christ, a former director of the Bible institute who served while we taught there, Bruce Hess, and one of the other missionaries from Bogotá all spoke. Both missionaries and Colombians sang. People from almost every Christian organization in Medellín were in attendance. It was really a beautiful service honoring Vernon.

The planning for Vernon's memorial service had to be done quickly, but it was done well. Our missionary friends contacted some people, and others volunteered just minutes before the service began.

We laid Vernon to rest in Campos de Paz, which is a beautiful cemetery that overlooks the city of Medellín.

As often happens in situations like this, I learned about how God was working and taking care of details after the crisis was over. Word had been sent by phone to the OMS headquarters in Greenwood, Indiana, on Sunday afternoon after Bruce received the news of Vernon's accident. On Monday morning, when the staff arrived at OMS headquarters, the message was immediately given to OMS President Dr. Wesley Duewel. Vernon's passing was announced at 8:00 to the staff, which was almost the same time I received my first phone contact that day. When I answered the second phone call, the people at OMS headquarters were on their knees, praying for the children and me.

After the funeral, I went back to the mission compound in Medellin. Up until that time, contacting our parents in the United States had been impossible. Getting a call through to the States was often difficult and could take hours. One of the missionaries helped by making the time-consuming phone connection with my parents while I gave undivided attention to our three precious children. As soon as my mother was on the line, the missionary handed the phone to me. I found out that

155

Dr. Duewel had already called my pastor and asked him to take word to my parents. Mother did not hesitate with her response when her pastor delivered the sad news. She said, "Let's pray for Millie and the children."

Dr. Duewel also contacted Vernon's family through Vernon's youngest sister's husband. Vernon's sister was teaching, so her husband waited until school was out to give her the news. They immediately went to the house of Vernon's mother.

I purposely waited to call Vernon's mother until I knew his sister, who was living at home, would be home from work. Vernon's older sister, Joyce Hintz, was a nurse and had just returned to work after taking off several weeks to care for their father in those last days of his life. I knew it would be especially hard for his mother because she had buried Vernon's father just three weeks earlier. Again, they already knew because Dr. Duewel made sure they received the news in a timely and appropriate manner.

The message from Dr. Duewel to both my parents and Vernon's mother was this, "Vernon Young, traveling to visit a congregation and a school, while crossing a stream, fell into the arms of Jesus."

The missionaries learned of Vernon's passing through a miracle worked by God. The only reason they found out anything at all was that the military base at Cimitarra called a military base in Medellín. They said a foreigner had died, and they were waiting for someone to identify him and bury him. No one at the military base had any idea who he was. All they knew was that he was a foreigner and an evangelical. One of the military personnel in Medellín said he had a friend who was an evangelical pastor. He volunteered to contact the pastor to see if he might know the identity of the body.

As only God can arrange such things, Vernon and I had taught that pastor at the Peniel Bible Institute. Arcesio immediately thought it had to be Vernon. They called him Varon, which in Spanish was man. That was as close to Vernon's name as they could get. Without hesitation, Arcesio called Bruce Hess. Bruce took that call at 2:30 Sunday afternoon.

Bruce and Arcesio tried to learn more, but their calls were not productive, as they could not get through to the people who could give them any information. The next morning they were able to discover a little more information, but no one seemed to know the location of the body. They were given two possibilities—Cimitarra or Puerto Berrio. We eventually found him at Cimitarra.

Vernon's tragic accident happened on February 6. The Mission in Medellín learned of his passing on February 8. On February 10, we took possession of his body, held a funeral service, and buried him.

Those were two excruciatingly difficult days. We took three special air flights, prayed for hours, waited through times of frustration, and experienced support from so many people. Our friends gathered together, remembering God's love and recalling Vernon's activities as he served God in this life as a living sacrifice. For us all, Vernon is now a beautiful memory to God's work in Colombia.

Actually, Vernon had four memorial services. Of course, there was the one in Medellín that the children and I attended. Our friends at Peniel Bible Institute held a service. My family at my home church in Wichita, Kansas, held a service. And Vernon's family at his home church in Appleton, Wisconsin, held a service.

A local pastor's wife and I invited people to come to the Mission compound at 2:30 the Sunday after Vernon's funeral service to share as pastors and leaders. I cannot express in words the beauty of the expressions of love and the lessons learned through this experience.

Everyone learned something. We realized more definitively that we never know when it is our time. One of the pastors stated so frankly and sincerely, "Vernon Young was carrying a responsibility and ministry that we ourselves as Colombians would not be willing to do. The hardships as well as the call to minister, in the way he did, would not be what we would choose for ourselves. But this speaks to us all. We must be ready to line up and carry the standard forward in our area as well as many other areas where a witness is needed."

One of the reasons I wanted to have this gathering was that I wanted to witness to these dear friends about how God's love had been evident to me during the past week. Yes, it was a time of great pain, but it was also a time of incredible love. So many of God's servants had demonstrated his love through the way they lovingly cared for Vernon's body, for our parents, for my children, and for me. I wanted them to know that our loving God had actually prepared me for that week. He had, through circumstances and through revelation during my devotional times, led me to understand the possibility that Vernon would not live a long life.

I stayed with friends in Medellín for about two weeks to complete the mountain of paperwork. At that time, I told the mission leadership that I was willing to stay in Magangué and carry on the work there until someone would be able to take it over. I served in Magangué until December of 1976. After those 10 months, I returned to Medellín.

Much later, when I was in the United States on home ministry assignment, Vernon's sister Joyce and I were reminiscing about Vernon. Joyce related that the family was a bit put out that Vernon had stayed only a week after his father's death. However, she clearly remembered the day of January 17, while the family was gathered at their parents' home. Vernon walked over to a group of pictures and picked up the picture of Colleen. Vernon said, "My dear Colleen. Colleen's birthday is today."

Joyce said, "It was obvious that Vernon could hardly wait to get back to Colombia to be with you and his children. Millie, you meant so much to Vernon. You made life such a beautiful thing for him from the time you were married."

*****

Millie's insight: Even Jesus wept when he learned of Lazarus's death, but there is still resurrection.

The winning Bible Quiz team. Millie organized Bible Quiz teams and competitions during her first term in Colombia

Manuel Moreno was the champion of the Bible Quiz team competition during the youth convention.

Millie rides into Galindo in style.

Vernon and Millie's wedding at Peniel Bible Institute

Millie waits for a boat with her suitcases and boxes containing the first Christmas gifts from Compassion International to the river children.

Ed Kimble of Compassion International (far left) and Millie (far right) at Puerto Claver School on the Cauca River

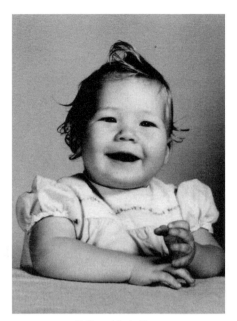

Colleen Marie Young

Joyce Ann Young

162

Joyce, Colleen, Millie, Vernon, and a Colombian girl on a boat deep in the river area of Colombia. On this trip, Colleen and Joyce joyfully sang, "With Christ in the vessel, you can smile at the storm."

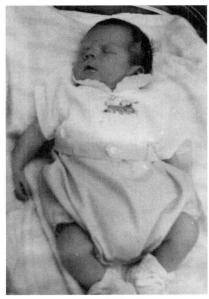

Howard Allen Young

The last family picture before God called Vernon home. The woman who took this picture in January 1976 was on a mission trip. She gave it to Vernon's sister after his death.

Millie speaks at the annual OMS Convention in Greenwood, Indiana.

*Colleen Young and
Graham Higgs wed.*

*Joyce Young and
Aldo Reusche wed.*

*Howard receives his masters of
clinical medical science from
Barry University in Miami.*

J.B. Crouse presents Millie with a plaque in recognition of her 49 years of missionary service with One Mission Society.

Millie continued leading Men for Missions teams to Colombia for many years after her official retirement.

CHAPTER TWENTY-THREE

None of These Things Move Me

"But none of these things move me, neither count I my life dear unto myself, so that I might finish my course with joy, and the ministry which I have received of the Lord Jesus, to testify the gospel of the grace of God." Acts 20:24 (KJV)

*****

Millie's insight: We may be hurt but not moved by what happens to us.

*****

The only Christians in the house were my maid and me, but this was not unusual. On February 6, 1976, a group of young people from the town of Magangué gathered in my home for our regular Friday night Bible study. They were interested in the Gospel but were not believers yet. That evening, we studied John 11, which is the story of the death and resurrection of Lazarus.

The evening Bible study had been routine, and everything was normal in the house. The children were sleeping, and I was tired. Normally on such an evening, I would quickly fall asleep. But that night was different. Inexplicably, my thoughts kept focusing on Vernon. I wondered how I would get word if something happened to him. My mind would not let that thought go. This did not make sense to me, as Vernon often took trips into the remote areas, and I had not suffered with sleeplessness

167

before. I thought I was being crazy. Why was I even thinking like that? It was a very long, restless night. As I reflected later, I realized God was preparing me for what I was to face in just a few days.

Quite often, I had house guests for one reason or another. Of course, they were always included in my morning devotions. On that particular morning, a teacher on her way to a school assignment, a young woman who helped with office work, my maid, and another woman were part of the devotional time. I read Psalm 43. I had read Psalm 42 the morning before. Strangely, the final verses in both chapters are identical.

> Why are you downcast, O my soul
> Why so disturbed within me?
> Put your hope in God,
>   for I will yet praise him,
>   my Savior and my God. (Psalm 42:11)

In addition, I read from Lettie Cowman's devotional book, *Streams in the Desert*. She wrote, "… yet our business is to hope in God, and it will be found that it is not in vain. In the Lord's own time help will come."[5]

During our devotional time on February 8, the reading from *Streams in the Desert* focused on Matthew 28:20: "… lo, I am with you always …" She included this quote from J. Hudson Taylor, "The Lord is my shepherd. Not was, not may be, nor will be. The Lord is my shepherd and he is on Sunday, is on Monday, and is through every day of the week; is in January, is in December, and every month of the year; is at home, and is in China; is in peace, and is in war; in abundance, and in penury."[6] I placed special emphasis on the word "is" each time I came to it, for the Lord IS my shepherd.

I went around the table that morning, speaking to each individual. To the maid I said, "The Lord **is** with your children." To the young woman helping me with office work, I said, "The Lord **is** with your mother." To another I said, "The Lord **is** with your family." I went all the way around the table. Then I ended with the statement, "The Lord **is** with Vernon. It is not Jesus was or he will be, but that he **is**."

Then on February 9, I received the phone call a few minutes

168

before 8:00 a.m. That morning, again, I had read, "Yet shall I praise him." This is when we see Paul saying that none of these things move him. He didn't say that they did not hurt him but that he would not be moved. So when word came about Vernon's accident, I quickly realized that God had been preparing me for what I was to hear.

One of the first questions I was asked after Vernon's funeral, even by some of our missionaries, was, "Millie, when can we come and help you pack? You will be going home, right?"

My response to these expressions of concern was, "Please, let me go back to what is now home and seek God's leading. We as a family must know what is right to do. And I want to be loyal to Christ and to have his smile upon me."

After Vernon's funeral it took several days to complete the legal paperwork required by Colombia and the United States. During that time in Medellín, I tried to make the necessary decisions and experience my grief. Then my children and I traveled home to Magangué where we returned to normal living and mission activities as best we could. About 10 days after arriving back, I met one of the teachers while on my way to pick up the mail. He was from the little village of La Hamaca. He was carrying the big box of school supplies I had sent to him. He said, "I guess we will not be having school now since Vernon is gone." When he learned of Vernon's death, he had boxed up the school supplies so they could be returned since he assumed the school would not be able to stay open.

That morning in my private devotions, I read Revelation 3:7b-8, which says, "What he opens no one can shut, and what he shuts no one can open. I know your deeds. See, I have placed before you an open door that no one can shut. I know that you have little strength, yet you have kept my word and have not denied my name."

I looked at that dear teacher and said, "Just this morning the Lord assured me that he had opened the doors to the little schools, and no one could shut them." The Lord had opened the door for me to go into Colombia in 1955. He had opened the door for us in 1975 to go to Magangué. Only he could shut those doors.

169

A few days later, I received a card that had been sent to Vernon in sympathy for the death of his father. In it was a poem. Even though the poem was sent to Vernon, these three stanzas were especially meaningful to me.

I am home in Heaven, dear ones;
　All's so happy, all's so bright!
There's perfect joy and beauty
　In this everlasting light.

There is work still waiting for you,
　So you must not idle stand;
Do your work while life remaineth
　You shall rest in Jesus' land.

When that work is all completed,
　He will gently call you home;
Oh, the rapture of the meeting!
　Oh, the joy to see you come![7]
　　　　—Author Unknown

The Bible Society had published this poem in a tract. The card and poem were sent by an old Chinese woman whom Vernon's sister Fern had led to the Lord. Fern had met the woman while she worked at a publishing company in Chicago. The woman had thoughtfully sent the card and poem to Vernon as an expression of sympathy and concern. To be honest, I could almost hear Vernon saying the first verse.

Before long I began to see that there was too much work for me to handle alone. I talked to the mission and to the national church about locating help. We were unable to find either a Colombian or a missionary to serve in the ministry efforts based in Magangué. We decided that I would move back to Medellín. It was not an easy decision.

So I made a trip to visit four of the schools that were not too far out. I took the three children along. It was an interesting trip because in every place that I shared, I felt the Lord was leading us to move back to Medellín. At each place, the believers said almost the same thing. They said, "Mildred, we understand, but know that when any of us come to Medellín, you will be the first one we look up. And we know you will keep working with us."

That was perhaps the turning point for me. I began to realize that it really was God's will for me to return to Medellín. Interestingly enough, in the next four years, the number of schools increased from 13 to 33.

In Medellín, my girls would attending George Washington School, where I had taught when I first started working in Colombia. So that my daughters could connect with the children at George Washington School, I sent them to Medellín ahead of Howard and me. Sending them early allowed them to be in the Christmas program and to participate in Christmas activities. It would aid in helping them feel a part of the school. They had only attended school in the little classroom I had set up in our apartment. The girls had been making many adjustments. My mother's heart was touched when, during the preparations for Joyce and Colleen to leave Magangué, Joyce sat down in tears one night. She asked, "If we leave, who will tell these people about Jesus?" So there was the burden, even with the children, of who was going to carry on the work.

I had everything packed in steel drums. It was mid-December by the time we moved. While waiting for the truck to arrive to pick up our things, I went to the rooftop to look out as Vernon and I had almost exactly two years before. I looked at the Magdalena River going all the way across in both directions. I said, "God, I commit your people into your hands. You have led us this far with them, and you will lead them on."

*****

"Put your hope in God for I will yet praise him,
my Savior and my God." Psalm 42:5b

*****

Millie's insight: We can hope in God at all times. We can still rejoice. He is our shepherd every day, month, year, and at all times. Wherever we are and in whatever circumstance, God so wonderfully prepares us if we will only listen to him.

171

CHAPTER TWENTY-FOUR

On Stage

"A gift is as a precious stone in the eyes of him that hath it."
Proverbs 17:8a (KJV)

*****

Millie's insight: We often hide our gifts. I believe God wants us to use the precious gifts he has given us.

*****

Play-acting was a common activity for rural Colombian children. They seemed to be quite gifted at improvising and acting out situations. I found their acting ability and their enthusiasm when acting to be a blessing. The students with whom I worked showed amazing talent in portraying the Word of God. They didn't need elaborate costumes and fancy props nor did they need a written script. They just acted the story. These talented young people would study the information presented in the Bible and then accurately portray the message on stage. They had an uncanny ability to bring the story to life for each member of the audience. Often the whole audience would be in tears at the end of a performance.

Until I married Vernon, my roommate at Peniel Bible Institute was Mary Joiner. Mary loved the acting ability of the Colombians and did all she could to encourage this expression

173

of their love for Jesus Christ. Whenever Mary traveled to the United States, she would return with her suitcases full of costumes for the students to use at the Bible institute—not stuff for herself. While making preparations to present a drama, the students knew that our door was open. The students would get a variety of costumes and props from us.

One time, the students were going to portray the story of Hagar when she took Ishmael and left Abraham and Sarah because of Sarah's inability to agree with Hagar's behavior toward her. The students came to our house and requested some props and costumes. We asked what they needed. The students said they needed a suitcase, an iron, an ironing board, and cosmetics. We did not ask what the students were going to do with cosmetics, an iron, and an ironing board in a portrayal of a biblical story, but we wondered how the students would use those items. They then selected costumes for the actors.

That night during the performance, the actors put the cosmetics in the suitcase, they ironed dresses, folded the dresses, and placed them in the suitcase. Then Hagar and Ishmael started their journey. Exhausted, they sat down under a nearby tree. Hagar said, "I'll just sit here and watch Ishmael die." The student actors successfully brought the story to life as a modern-day portrayal of an Old Testament event.

These dramas brought the audience to an understanding of how the Scriptures applied to their lives. They used Scripture in the presentations and made it alive with meaning. After a presentation, Mary and I often sat and laughed from pure enjoyment at the creativity of our beloved Colombian students. We would say to ourselves, "This probably would not go over in the U.S."

One year, I decided it would be great fun to have a drama as a final program before the little primary school let out for the summer break. Because they were studying Colombian history, I selected a topic that would appeal to the national spirit of the children and parents. Even in the rural areas, the Colombian people are quite patriotic. They love their country in spite of all their hardships. This is one of the characteristics of the Colombian people that I especially appreciate.

174

The students and teachers both took part in the production portraying Colombia's liberation. One of the major characters was Simón Bolívar. He is a hero of the Colombian people much like George Washington is a hero in the United States.

The students worked for weeks, getting everything ready. From practice to practice, the script was perfected. The students were so excited about their drama that they even invited the people from the village to the performance of their patriotic program.

During one of the final rehearsals, the student playing Simón Bolívar approached me. He pointed out that Simón Bolívar rode a white horse, and the mission compound had a white horse. He wanted to ride that horse to the chapel for his grand entrance. I said, "Well, I guess you can ride the white horse down the hill to the chapel, but you cannot ride the horse into the chapel."

"Oh no!" came the reply. "I'll leave the horse at the door." I granted permission.

During the final rehearsal, he rode the white horse down to the chapel. He stopped the horse close to the sidewalk. I became concerned and cautioned him. "Numael, you are going to be riding the horse at a run down the hill. Now you are going to want to be sure you do not let the horse on the concrete because it is shoed. If it hits that concrete with those shoes on, it will fall." Numael understood. He was a kid from way out in the country, and he assured me he knew what he was doing. We practiced one time with the horse to make sure instructions were understood.

The night of the program arrived. The signal for Simón Bolívar to ride the horse to the door of the chapel to make his grand entrance was a flashlight waving from the door. About half the people from the village were curious why someone was leaving the building with a flashlight and signaling. So they followed to be sure they were not missing anything. Was there an intruder? A robber? What was happening? This presented a problem for the actors. Simón would not be able to enter through the crowd. So as the crowd was being ushered back to their seats, someone ran up the hill to tell Simón to wait a minute. The light was flashed again. He came flying down the hill. In the excitement, the horse ran onto the concrete and fell. Its front feet were splayed out in front of it. Horse and rider slid through the open chapel door. The people sitting on the benches by the door jumped up on their benches.

Now you would think this would have stopped the drama. But no, this quick-thinking youngster spread his feet out in the stirrups to prevent them from getting caught under the horse. Simón Bolívar was in full character and not going to let a horse falling and sliding through the open chapel doors interrupt his performance. When the horse came to a stop, he dismounted and marched to the front of the chapel with a straight, authoritative posture. He was in character during the whole incident, treating it as if it was a planned part of the performance.

A couple of the men helped me get the horse back up on its feet and marched it out the other side of the chapel as Simón went strutting down the aisle. Luckily the horse was not injured, nor did it act like it was too excited about the whole experience. Actually, the audience hardly noticed the horse's exit because as Simón marched down the aisle, the audience spontaneously erupted in chanting, "Simón Bolívar! Simón Bolívar!"

The main part of the performance went as planned. However, at the end, as Simón marched down the aisle to exit the drama, everyone in the audience fell in behind him marching as they chanted, "Long live Simón Bolívar!"

As I reflect on that dramatic experience, no play could have been written, or performed for that matter, that would have brought as much attention and audience involvement as happened that night. The audience was emotionally drawn into the performance. It was as if Simón Bolívar was alive and in their presence.

I cannot help but laugh every time I think about that dramatic performance. Even years later, whenever I met up with Numael, we always had a hearty laugh about that night.

I am sure that the poor rural Colombians' dramatic ability is a God-given talent that they perfect from the time they are very little as they play. Because of their extreme poverty, the children have to be creative because they have no toys. They may have a corncob to use as a car or, if it is hollowed out, they might pretend it is a canoe. The little girls do not have dolls. They have to improvise and pretend as they entertain themselves.

Gilma, one of the women who worked at the Christian high school, and I were talking the last time I led a work team in the area. Gilma told me that she never had a toy when she was growing up. At Christmas time it was a special treat when her mother would buy eggs, fry them, and divide them so each family member could have a fourth of a fried egg. But she did not feel that she was deprived. She was not complaining but just stating facts.

The students at Peniel Bible Institute lived together, studied together, created dramas together, played together, and ate together. They had a real community. When the end of the term arrived and they prepared to return to their home communities, they were heartbroken because of the impending separation. The night before leaving was a night of no sleep. They cried. They sang songs like "In the Sweet By and By" and "God Be With You Till We Meet Again." They recounted stories from the months they had spent together. The next morning they would all go down the hill to the train station with their suitcases made of cardboard or flattened tin cans.

Current wisdom in the United States is that children must have modern conveniences, planned intellectual stimulation, and opportunities designed to develop their talents. The rural Colombian children are taught to swim while they are babies as their mothers bathed them in the rivers. Their brains are challenged and creativity is developed as they explored their environment and find ways to entertain themselves. The poor rural Colombian people may be economically impoverished, but they are very creative, loving, and intelligent.

*****

Millie's insight: May we use our God-given talents to serve our master.

177

CHAPTER TWENTY-FIVE

Prayer Changes
Sincere Prayer Affects Others

"The prayer of a righteous man is powerful and effective."
James 5:16b

*****

Millie's insight: Day or night, you can receive a burden to pray for a missionary on the field. A name may come to you even if you are not very familiar with that missionary. If a missionary is placed before you, God knows the need at that time. Your prayer is important.

*****

One year had passed since my husband's accidental death. I made plans to visit a school and church in the remote area where he had been traveling. I planned to take my 2 daughters and a group of 29 teenagers who were participating in a mission trip through the OMS youth program. I had made arrangements for three-year-old Howard to stay with a local missionary family. Joyce, who was now seven, looked forward to the trip, but nine-year-old Colleen flatly refused to travel back into the rural areas because it was extremely frightening to her. Colleen fully understood her father's death had happened when he fell from a horse while traveling out there. The dangers of jungle travel were

179

very real to her. Reluctantly, I talked with the family who had agreed to care for Howard while I was leading the short-term mission group. That dear family was willing to let Colleen stay with them also.

Little did I know that God had laid it upon the hearts of a group of people in western Canada to pray for me. One of the OMS prayer warrior leaders was traveling through Canada. She needed a place to stay for the night and called one of her friends to see if she could stay at her home. This friend was a faithful member of an OMS prayer group that held regular monthly prayer meetings to pray for OMS missionaries and programs. At the beginning of the prayer meeting that same evening that Colleen was refusing to travel into the jungle, God laid it upon the heart of someone at the meeting to pray for my children and me.

The visiting prayer leader wondered what had happened to me. After the prayer meeting, she anxiously asked if the group had any new information about us. She knew that Vernon had died in a tragic accident and was concerned for my safety. The answer was that they had no updates. They were just led by the Holy Spirit to pray purposefully for me.

That same day in Colombia, I went about taking care of the last-minute details for the trip and preparing the teens for the mission activities planned for the next few days. Both Joyce and Colleen had enjoyed the time with the high school students as they were given orientation training for the trip. The young people doted over the two girls, and the girls relished telling stories to the teens. Both Joyce and Colleen were great story-tellers and didn't hesitate to embellish the truth a bit for special effect. The exciting stories were fun for both the tellers and the listeners. But Colleen still did not want to have anything to do with venturing into the rural areas because her father had died while traveling out there.

On Thursday evening, as I was finishing up last minute details for breakfast the next morning, Colleen evidently was having a tentative change of heart as she asked me if she could change her mind about going on the mission trip. Even though this pleased me, I told Colleen that she would have to pack a

180

suitcase whether she stayed with friends or boarded the train with me. Colleen could make her final decision the next morning.

To my surprise, Colleen did not change her mind. She was up early, helped with breakfast, and generally seemed somewhat excited about the trip. Colleen had a dramatic change of attitude—refusal, then tentative possibility, to enthusiastic participant. I had no idea what had triggered the difference, but I thanked the Lord and continued with my responsibilities.

It was not a short train trip even though we only had to travel 100 miles. The train stopped at every village along the way, so it took almost nine hours to reach our destination. The train was on a narrow gauge track, so it rocked a lot. It was a noisy affair, and talking very loudly was essential if one wanted to be heard. Of course, I tried to point out features of Colombia and the life of rural Colombians to the young people. After all, part of their trip was to gain knowledge about the indigenous people. My voice was feeling the strain before we reached our destination at Puerto Parra where OMS had established a church and school.

By the time the evening worship service was to begin, my voice was gone. The plan was for the youth to give their testimonies; however, they only spoke English. I could not speak loudly enough to be heard since a sound system wasn't available. Both Colleen and Joyce were fluent in Spanish and English, so everyone encouraged Colleen to act as interpreter. She did an amazing job of listening to the English testimonies and translating them into Spanish then listening to the Spanish comment or question and translating it into English. It was a successful evening due to the language skills of nine-year-old Colleen.

The next day, the youth divided into three groups for door-to-door visitation. Local youth joined the teams. Joyce, Colleen, and I went along to act as interpreters. The youth from both cultures became quick friends as they invited people to the evening service and passed out tracts. Both of my daughters felt like they were an important part of the groups and enjoyed all the attention they received. The success of the trip was largely because of their translating skills.

181

Just before the group boarded the train Sunday afternoon, the local believers asked me to return in October and bring "Little Vernon." They had enjoyed the girls and wanted to meet my youngest child. They had known and loved Big Vernon. He had worked for Compassion International in coordination with OMS to establish a Christian day school in this river town. The people in the areas where Vernon worked had a special heart for him and his family.

As we were boarding the train to return home Sunday afternoon, I could hardly hold back the tears when Colleen told me that she wanted to come back with me when I returned to Puerto Parra. Colleen had a complete change in attitude. God had truly worked in her heart.

I did not know about the OMS prayer meeting, in which prayers were centered on my children and me, until three years later at an OMS convention in the United States. That traveling Canadian prayer warrior sought me out and asked to know what the need was for my family and me during the time that she had attended the prayer meeting when I had been laid on the hearts of the people in that OMS prayer group. I was uncertain what the crisis had been, but I knew it had to have been important to God since that little prayer team had fervently prayed for my children and me.

When I arrived home after the convention and looked at some of my notes for that date, I discovered the prayer group had been praying during the exact time Colleen had decided she would go on the trip into the jungle with the high school youth mission team.

*****

Millie's insight: When God leads, may we not sin against him by failing to pray for those that he asks us to pray for.

CHAPTER TWENTY-SIX

I Signed Up for This?

"But you will receive power when the Holy Spirit comes on you; and you will be my witnesses in Jerusalem, and in all Judea and Samaria, and to the ends of the earth." Acts 1:8

*****

Millie's insight: Training new personnel to take the torch and carry out the Great Commission is of utmost importance.

*****

Four years after Vernon's fatal accident, Gail Leroy, a former missionary kid, came to Colombia with a seven-day youth mission trip. However, Gail felt the Lord was telling her to extend her stay to one month.

A petition for an extended stay is not often granted because of the challenges of mission work. But her request was approved since she had lived on the mission field as a child. After the team left, she worked with me in Medellín. Having her help was a blessing as there was so much to do for those little schools because they had increased in number. It was a wonderful opportunity to encourage Gail to follow God's leading. She understood that God was calling her to the mission field.

Because Gail was a missionary kid, she had a better understanding than most beginning missionaries of the trials and tribulations of life on the mission field. The time she had spent after high school ministering with me to the Colombians in the remote villages had uniquely prepared her. However, she was soon to learn first-hand that the life of a missionary could sometimes be unpredictable.

I was responsible for Gail's missionary training. One "field trip" experience is etched into my memory. I needed to make a trip to encourage teachers and update records for the rural schools. This was to be a trip to begin training Gail to assume some of the responsibilities in the areas we would visit. The plan was for Gail to work beside me as I instructed her. I would tell her this is the way you do this and the way you do that. I was teaching her the ministry of the small, rural schools, as well as the work that we had to do for Compassion International to satisfy the requirements for the scholarships they provided. It was supposed to be a practical training trip.

I preferred to take my children with me on trips to the rural areas when possible. I enjoyed having them with me, and my children enjoyed the adventure. However, I was unable to leave at the designated departure time because of a school responsibility of one of the girls. So I sent Gail to the first location two days ahead of me. I believed Gail could competently get started without me being present at the first school. Because Gail did not know the area well, she flew to the designated location.

I decided to go by bus because it was much less expensive to purchase bus tickets than plane tickets for one adult and three children. My children and I would travel overnight and arrive in the early morning where Gail was to be. We would finish up whatever she had not completed and proceed to the next school location.

The bus had barely left Medellín when it stopped to take on new passengers, which was customary. People waited on the side of the road for the bus to arrive, and the bus stopped when it came upon anyone waiting. A bus employee, called the *déle* boy, collected the fares as the bus resumed its trip. Unfortunately, these two new passengers were about as drunk as they could get and still be able to stand up. Because the bus was almost full, the déle boy told the men they would have to sit in

184

the back of the bus. They staggered toward the rear seats.

When the déle boy went back to collect their fare, the men objected. They were not about to pay any fare. The two men then got into a fight between themselves, while at the same time, they were both angry with the déle boy. There I was with three young children, and these drunk men were flailing away at each other and anyone else who was near. They were fighting and falling all over the passengers, including my children. This was very disturbing to Colleen. She had had enough of their bad behavior.

Quite some time passed before the bus arrived at a little filling station where we could halt. The déle boy got off the bus, and the two drunk men followed after him. But on the way off the bus, they grabbed a couple of machetes from the luggage racks and went after the driver and the déle boy. The men went into the filling station and grabbed chairs. They emerged, swinging their machetes and flinging the chairs about. They even attacked the bus with the machetes and made gashes on the sides of the bus.

The men terrorized the passengers with their behavior. I ended up on the floor with my three children under me as I tried to protect them. I had no idea what was going to happen next.

The driver and the déle boy emerged from the filling station. The driver jumped into the bus and took off. It looked like he was driving across a field. I could not see where he was going as it was pitch dark. He was driving like mad. As people started to get up and sit in their seats, they realized the two drunk men were not on the bus, but neither was the déle boy. Someone started yelling, "You left the déle boy!" But the driver just kept on driving. I thought, *Oh my lands, I think he did leave that poor déle boy behind.*

Eventually we came to a little town. Just as we approached the town, people started calling, "*Los micos! Los micos!*" A car was approaching from behind the bus. The people were yelling that those monkeys had followed us. They were fearful that the two men had found a car and were chasing us. I jumped off the bus and was trying to find a safe place to hide. I was determined to protect my children. I saw a nearby house and thought that I might be able to convince the owners to let me in until the men were gone. Just as I reached the door I turned around because I heard everyone laughing. At first, I thought they might be laughing at me. But no. They were laughing out of relief as they realized that the men weren't in the car. So the *micos* were not coming. What a blessing!

Most of the luggage was stored on top of the bus under a tarp. Once he knew it was safe, the déle boy emerged from under that tarp. I have no idea how he managed to get to the top of the bus and under the tarp during that frantic, bumpy ride from the filling station as we sped away from the danger the drunk men presented. He apparently grabbed the ladder on the side of the bus as it raced away from the filling station and crawled onto the roof, hiding among the secured luggage. What an uncomfortable ride he must have experienced, but at least he was unharmed and alive.

The children and I boarded the bus again. During the early morning hours, we traveled through an area where the road was wet and boggy. The bus became stuck in the quagmire. This was frustrating because we were close to our destination. Everyone had to get off the bus and walk ahead. The bus driver hoped that this would make the bus light enough to get it out of the mud hole. I trudged through the mud with my three tired children. We had experienced a long night with almost no sleep.

During this muddy trek, a friendly Colombian walked up beside Colleen and said, "You were kind of scared back there."

Her youthful reply was, "You would have been scared, too, if you had been burned with a cigarette butt!" Colleen was not a happy traveler right then.

We had to walk quite a distance before the bus was on ground solid enough to allow the passengers to get back on board. All of the travelers had extremely muddy feet. We were just filthy by the time we were able to board the bus.

Finally we arrived at El Barge, where Gail was waiting for us. The children and I were exhausted, but we had work to do. There was no time to rest. I worked with Gail all that day, taking care of the essential tasks before we departed for the next

186

location on the itinerary. As we worked, we described to each other our experiences from the night before. She had also had a sleepless night.

The parsonage where Gail was staying behind the OMS church had a tin roof. She understood that missionaries not only eat whatever is given them, but they also sleep wherever they are given a place to sleep. However, she was not comfortable with the sleeping arrangement, as she had heard a frightening scratching noise on the tin roof all night long.

With a little chuckle, I said, "Gail, do you know what that was? It was vultures."

Gail erupted, "Vultures!"

After laughing at her typical outspoken response, I explained, "This is a fishing port. When the men return from fishing, they clean the fish on the shore. Then the vultures eat the fish carcasses and entrails that have been tossed on the ground. The vultures wait on the roof all night for the men to return with their catch of fish the next morning."

Because of the noise of the vultures roosting on the tin roof, no one had much sleep that night either. But the lack of sleep was not going to stop us from doing what we had set out to do on this trip.

The next morning, we left on a river launch to Puerto Claver. A river launch is a rectangular wooden boat that usually has low sides and a top to provide shade from the sun.

We arrived at the home where we were to stay. A little wooden casket containing the body of a young child was sitting on the family table because one of the children in that family had died during the night. Eleven-year-old Colleen was old enough to understand that a dead body was in the casket and that in a few hours she would be sitting at that same table, eating a meal. This was almost more that her young mind could handle. On this trip, she had witnessed a drunken brawl, waded through an enormous expanse of mud, slept under vultures, had very little sleep, and now she would be expected to eat a meal at a table on which a casket with a dead child in it had been placed only a short time before. Colleen's sensitivities had been invaded. As a missionary kid whose father had died in a tragic accident, she could not be considered a child sheltered from the realities of life. But this was almost too much.

However, that dear family had lost one of their precious children during the night. Because there was no embalming in the rural areas, a body had to be buried within 24 hours. The table was the most honorable place to set the casket until the burial later that morning.

Gail and I were able to easily complete all the necessary work at that location. We had some time before the evening worship service, so we decided to get everything ready for our departure the next morning. We would need to be up early and ready to leave at 4:30 on another river launch.

We set up our hammocks. Each one should have had two ropes to secure it, but somewhere along the way, we had lost a rope. Since one was missing, we decided to hang two hammocks with three ropes. Gail had been in Girl Scouts when she was younger and understood knots. She assured me she could safely hang two hammocks with three ropes. She said, "I've done this before. I can fix it." So Gail tied the ropes, and the hammocks were ready for us to sleep in after the church service.

We returned to the hammocks after church. I charged everyone to have everything handy for leaving the next morning. The only light we would have would be from a flashlight. Therefore, we needed to have everything packed, and what we would need in the morning had to be easily accessible so we could get ready quickly. The last instruction I gave was, "When I call you in the morning, hop right up."

Colleen and Gail slept in the two hammocks tied up with three ropes. They both crawled into their hammocks. Suddenly, Colleen said, "Oh, I forgot to brush my teeth." So, she hopped down from her hammock. When she did, Gail's hammock came crashing down. While we had been at the church, someone saw the way Gail had tied the hammocks and decided to tie them the "right way."

Colleen finished brushing her teeth, so into the newly secured hammock she went.

After a few minutes, Colleen started to say something. Gail

immediately interrupted her. "Don't you move. Just don't you move." Everyone burst out laughing. In a moment or two, Gail asked Colleen what she needed. Whatever it was, Colleen decided she really didn't need it after all.

I chuckled and then said, "All right. In the morning, when I call, Gail, will you be the first to get up?"

Gail replied, "No doubt about that Millie. The second I hear you, I'll be up."

The next morning we arose early, dressed, took down and packed the hammocks, and boarded our boat launch.

I definitely would rather sleep in a hammock when visiting rural areas. I have never had any trouble finding a location to hang my hammock. The rural structures had poles that were sturdy enough from which to hang a hammock. The beds found in rural areas were split bamboo placed on a frame, with the round side of the bamboo facing up. On top of the bamboo, they placed a straw sleeping mat. The mats were usually infested with bedbugs, which were very irritating little creatures. It was not advisable to sleep on the ground because of snakes and other creatures that are active during the night.

Galindo was our next destination. In this little village, we were to stay in the small church. The first night, we hung our hammocks in the church. Gail's hammock was hung in the hallway entrance of the church, while the children's hammocks and my hammock were hung in the open area of the sanctuary. I always tied Howard's hammock close to mine because when he was sleeping soundly, he snored. His snore sounded much like a motorcycle revving its engine. When he started making the roaring noise, I would shake his hammock, which usually worked to tame the noise.

Everyone had just dropped off to sleep when Gail jumped up and onto the floor. "Oh! Oh!" she exclaimed. Then she began to laugh. "I don't know what it was, but something was after me, and I jumped out of my hammock." After a good laugh about her action-filled dream, we all went back to sleep. Our trip had been full of many night adventures, and we needed rest to face the next day.

Since we were leaving early the following morning, we had

189

placed some food in a couple of plastic bags. We would grab the bags and eat while we floated on the river to our next location. The children from the village had brought us some delicious, huge, tree-ripened mangos. We had also purchased some clay-oven baked rolls from a lady. The bread baked in a rural clay oven is absolutely the best bread. We were all looking forward to a breakfast of mangos and rolls.

During the night, I was awakened from a sound sleep by scratching noises, which resembled crumpled paper being drug across the floor. I wondered what was happening. What could be causing that scratching sound? I grabbed the flashlight, which I always kept in my hammock on rural excursions. I flashed my light just in time to see a huge rat pulling our bag of bread out of the room. Close behind it was another huge rat pulling the bag with our mangos. Our breakfast was gone.

We arrived on the riverbank at the appointed time. It had rained most of the night, so the river was running swiftly, and river transportation was scarce. We waited and waited and waited. I knew it was common for river craft not to be timely, but when my children hadn't had anything to eat, it was difficult to wait. I walked over to a woman in a little hut on the riverbank. She was making coffee.

I asked her, "Would you by any chance be able to make a little cup of coffee for each one of us?" My motherly concern for my children to have something to eat must have been very strong as none of my children had drunk coffee before, and this coffee would be extremely strong and very sweet. In my desperation, I thought at least they would have a little something in their tummies. I paid her, and the woman made little demitasse cups of coffee for each of us.

The launch finally arrived at 10:00 a.m. When we arrived at Montecristo, our next destination, our only choice was to start working immediately because we had arrived much later than expected. Even if breakfast had been planned for us earlier, it was now well past eating time and nothing was offered. I helped Gail start taking the biannual data records for the Compassion International scholarship students. I told her that we were heading to the home of the woman in charge of accounting to review her books.

190

Just as I was leaving, Gail said. "Millie, come back. Is yellow fever contagious?"

I replied, "Oh, yes."

Before she even thought, Gail recorded "depart" on the report. She was going to take a child out of the program because she had yellow fever.

I decided maybe I needed to investigate. I said, "Wait just a minute, Gail. Let me talk to them." After a conversation with the teacher, I learned the young girl had hepatitis. That was what caused the yellow hue of her skin. I went on to explain to Gail that hepatitis is also contagious but not as much as yellow fever. We would just need to be sure we did not eat anything cooked in the little girl's house or drink water while we were there.

I discovered that the little girl lived in the house where I was going to check the accounting books. The work progressed well. The lady, sensing that I could use some refreshment, asked if I would like a cup of coffee. I was tired and hungry so I immediately responded, "Oh, yes. Thank you."

Gail looked at me and as soon as the lady left the room said, "I thought you were not going to eat or drink anything in this house." Gail had real concern for my health.

I replied, "I have already committed. I cannot change my mind now. It would offend her terribly. You do not need to drink any. Just tell her you do not want any coffee at this time." I politely drank the coffee and did not contract hepatitis.

I looked over at my children. They were cutting sugar cane with the little girl who had hepatitis, and they were using a knife from her home.

A very concerned Gail said, "You kids get that cane out of your mouth."

I calmly said, "Gail it's too late now." And it was. If that knife was going to expose them, they were exposed. I knew my children were hungry, so they were immensely enjoying the sweet treat. I felt so bad because I had no way to feed them. There wasn't even a place where I could buy them a little something to eat.

Finally, I was told they were preparing a lunch for us in

about an hour. I consoled my children with the knowledge that they would have a filling meal soon. So they played with the village children for a while.

Guaranda was the next destination. We were to stay in the school building, which had ample room to hang the hammocks. Somewhere along the way, we had obtained another rope. However, this time the problem was rain. The roof of the school leaked, and all night long the drips came constantly. Gail, the children, and I needed to change positions in our hammocks often to avoid the worst drips. Sometimes, we even turned around so that our heads were at the other end of the hammock. But my thoughts were not about my discomfort. I felt sorrow for the children who sat in this schoolroom during the rainy season and dodged the drips all day.

During the middle of that rainy night, the donkeys began to bray. One donkey had stationed itself next to the school door. It brayed constantly the rest of the night. The next morning, when my children woke, they sat up and, almost in unison, said, "That dumb donkey brayed all night long!" Then we all laughed.

Like all children, they had a bit of an adventurous spirit so they decided to have some fun out of the experience. They plotted during that morning, and I had no idea what they were conniving to do.

All day, Gail and I were busy collecting Compassion International applications for potential scholarship students. As a part of the process, each student had his picture taken with a board on which the number of the school and the number of that individual child were placed. Each application had the child's number on it. This was a simple and effective identification process.

My children thought it would be fun to give the donkey a scholarship. They held the number identification board in front of that donkey, and Gail snapped the picture. We sent the picture in with the case histories from the school to Compassion International headquarters in the United States. We stated on the application that this was the "student" that arrived at midnight and stayed in front of the door all the rest of the night, asking for entrance.

192

Compassion probably never had anything so silly done before. But for us, it was entertaining! The kids laughed and laughed, and they now had another fun story to tell about their adventures out on the rivers.

We had very little sleep during that trip. To say the least, Gail did receive realistic training. She took it all in, learned from it, and did not quit.

Gail is another treasure I encountered during my missionary experience.

*****

Millie's insight: Sometimes, it sounds like ministry was a lot of work; it was. But mission work is also a lot of fun. You have a lot of laughs and satisfaction. It is very gratifying when new workers take up the torch and go forward. The emotion is almost impossible to contain when you look back and see your disciples developing into real leaders, not just pastors and teachers, but true leaders of the national church, taking over responsibilities that for so many years were the missionaries' responsibilities.

CHAPTER TWENTY-SEVEN

Against All Odds
God's People Are the Real Treasure

"He told them, 'The harvest is plentiful, but the workers are few. Ask the Lord of the harvest, therefore, to send out workers into his harvest field.'" Luke 10:2

*****

Millie's insight: Many of the humble, underprivileged, rural Colombian people are precious treasures in kingdom work.

*****

Sometimes God uses a desire for something you cannot have to motivate you to do the impossible. That was the case with Tomás. He was an ordinary, underprivileged rural Colombian boy. He did not stand out. He expected, like most boys from his background, that his education would stop after completing fifth grade. As a matter of fact, he would be lucky to receive that much formal education because many did not.

The other missionaries and I knew if we could reach the children through our Christian primary day schools, our ministry to the Colombian people would be far more productive. The children would be able to read the Bible and receive the Gospel message at a young age. Because of this insight from the Lord, the missionaries in Colombia saw a need for not only more pastors to serve in the rural areas but also for training rural

195

young people to serve as Christian teachers.

The Peniel Bible Institute was started by OMS to provide believers with theological training to prepare them to be rural pastors, but it developed into a training location for pastors and teachers in the rural areas. Because of our experiences with the deep faith of rural believers, OMS used Genesis 32:30 as the basis for naming Peniel Bible Institute: "And Jacob called the name of the place Peniel: for I have seen God face to face, and my life is preserved." (KJV)

From 1962 through 1974, I devoted my life to preparing young people to become Christian primary teachers in the rural areas of Colombia. The effectiveness of the program was proven by the lives of Colombians such as Tomás.

During the time Tomás was growing up in a remote area, Peniel Bible Institute had raised its standards in an effort to improve the educational level of our graduates and to ensure we were attracting serious students. We started requiring that students had at least one year of high school education to qualify for enrollment at the Peniel Bible Institute. That meant they had to have one year beyond the fifth grade. The only way the other missionaries and I could find to provide these dear young people with the needed high school education was to start a Christian boarding dorm in the river port town of Magangué on the Magdalena River. Placing OMS dorms at that location would allow us to attract students from the Christian day schools located up and down the river.

The obstacles were huge. Buildings to serve as dorms would need to be found or built. The students probably would not be able to pay for their education. Dorm parents would need to be recruited and paid a salary. And no funds were available. Nevertheless, the Lord laid a strong burden on my heart to do something for the students who wanted a high school education. I knew that my dear husband, who had died only a year earlier, would enthusiastically support my efforts.

Some of the students from the rural Christian primary schools attended the public high schools, but that was not a very good solution because it was not uncommon for the public school teachers to be on strike for months at a time. So it sometimes took two or three years for the students to complete one year of education. Attending public high school was just not satisfactory. For that reason, we encouraged students who wanted to further their education to attend the private parochial Catholic high school in Magangué because it did not observe the public school teacher strikes. Although it was not ideal, it was the best option. We expected criticism, but my colleagues and I knew it was the only viable path at that time. Besides, these youngsters had been receiving quality Bible training through the day schools, the witness of the believers in communities, and the pastors who served in small local churches.

In November of 1973, Compassion International sent representatives to Colombia to visit six of the OMS Christian schools to determine how they could best help with the education of the Colombian children. They were specifically interested in providing scholarships for needy children to make sure they received an elementary education. Compassion International started financially assisting where I was working with the primary schools. In 1977, they agreed to help children attend high school even if it was not a Christian high school since none were available. But the children were required to attend church and Sunday school regularly and to show a genuine interest in the Gospel. Also, Compassion International agreed to provide some financial assistance in hiring a dorm mom.

One Mission Society was fortunate to hire a woman who was a graduate of the Peniel Bible Institute and had served as a teacher in one of the primary schools. She was one of the older teachers serving OMS schools and was very mature. Only boys were enrolled the first two years because we didn't have appropriate facilities or staff to supervise males and females in the same building. Two local girls were hired to help the dorm mom with cleaning, laundry, and cooking. For two years, this lovely woman made sure those teenage boys attended school on time, checked for completed homework, helped them with disagreements, and nursed them when they were sick.

The requests for entrance into the dorm were growing. We needed more than a dorm mother. We needed a couple to act as parents for the boys. At that time, I was doing pre-marriage counseling with a Christian teacher and his fiancée. The need for dorm parents came up in a normal conversation during one of our sessions. To my surprise, Teobaldo and Carmen Camargo were interested. Carmen had received her primary education in the small village of Colorado, and her family members were the charter members of the church there. Teobaldo was also a graduate of the Peniel Bible Institute. Two weeks after they were married, this young couple became dorm parents for 16 teenage boys.

A young boy named Tomás, whose parents were separated, lived in one of the little river port towns. He came from a large family, with 13 brothers and sisters. He was the sixth of nine boys. He had chosen to live with his father and help him farm at a location farther inland to assist in providing for the family.

Tomás had attended the Christian day school at the port village for two years. Because he helped his father farm, he missed attending school. He had been absent so much that he knew he would be placed in a class with much younger children if he chose to live with his mother and attend school. Even though he wanted more education, he was reluctant because he knew he would be teased for being so old and only in the third grade.

He finally decided to live with his mother and just endure the teasing so he could receive an education. Through the school Bible studies, he came to a saving faith in Jesus Christ. Someone had given his teacher several New Testaments to distribute to her students. Tomás took his faith seriously and read through his New Testament several times. During his fourth grade year, he studied in the morning and worked in the afternoon at whatever he could find to do for a little money. When he entered fifth grade, he became very discouraged. He desperately wanted to go to high school, but his father had lost both of his crops as a result of the flooding that year. They had no money for education. The family would need every cent to just survive.

At that time, OMS offered no Christian high school program. His only option was the public high school or a parochial school, but there was no public high school in his village. He would need money to pay for room and board to live in a village that had a high school, and of course a parochial school would require tuition payment. Neither were possibilities for him because of the crop failure that year.

One of the responsibilities of the dorm parents at the Christian dorm was to travel up and down the river to the Christian day schools for the purpose of discovering who desired to attend high school. On one of these trips, Teobaldo met Tomás. Teobaldo saw that Tomás had a real burden to attend high school, so he told him to go ahead and apply. He would see that Tomás would receive a scholarship. It was a statement of faith because OMS did not have a scholarship program for high school students at that time. Tomás was not a scholarship student through Compassion International from the school he attended, and the mission did not have means of providing for him. Neither did Teobaldo have the funds. However, Tomás found someone who would lend him enough money to pay for his boat ride to Magangué.

This situation solidified in my mind the need to get a scholarship program for those children who wanted to attend high school and had the talent to do well but lacked the funds to pay. I decided to approach OMS. I had met OMS vice president Dave Graffenberger when he was a young missionary, so I was comfortable with contacting him.

His first response was that it had not been done before, but Dave was willing to listen to my concern. I explained the situation and the burden the Lord had placed on my heart. OMS had set up Christian day schools and trained primary teachers to staff those schools. But once the children finished primary school, there was nothing for them to do. I explained that we currently required the students to have one year of high school but the requirements for acceptance into Peniel Bible Institute were being raised each year until six years of high school would be the entrance requirement. Many young people who demonstrated potential to be Christian teachers and preachers were not being trained because they could not afford to attend high school. "What are we to do?" was my question. Dave understood the worthiness of my proposal. He told me to write it up and send it to OMS headquarters. He would back me.

Dave traveled to Colombia to get a firsthand look at the OMS mission projects. That trip solidified his support for my proposal. He developed a heart for the education of the Colombian young people and whole-heartedly supported the proposal to provide scholarships for promising young people to attend high school. OMS agreed that if the missionaries could raise the money, the scholarship program could proceed. Because of this decision, we were able to give Tomás the help he needed that first year. Teobaldo advised Tomás to not let economic problems keep him

199

from his studies because God would provide. And God did just that in a miraculous and surprising way.

Tomás worked during the summer in an effort to raise funds for his education. He even tried panning gold. He did not make very much. He came with about $8 in his pocket. At the end of the next summer, because Teobaldo knew Tomás and another student would arrive a few days late for school, he was concerned that the priest running the local parochial school would not accept them. The priest said it would be okay if the two students were coming from one of the OMS Christian day schools. According to that priest, the students from our little Christian schools were the best students he had. He told Teobaldo that the morals of the OMS students were unbelievable, the students got along with people, and they were intelligent. What a joy it was for the missionaries and dorm parents to hear those words!

Tomás received a big surprise when he arrived a few days late at school for his second year of high school. The priest had started a new program of offering a full scholarship to the student who had the highest grade-point average of the entire high school the past school year. When they figured the grade averages, that student was Tomás. He loved his studies, and he worked hard. He did amazingly well all the years he attended that school, earning that full academic scholarship for five years in a row. Of course, he was valedictorian of his graduating class.

To be a part of the high school graduation ceremonies, boys were required to wear black trousers and a white long-sleeved shirt, regular shoes (not sandals), and socks. Tomás had maybe $2 or $3—not close to enough money to purchase the required clothing.

Near the time for graduation, Tomás approached Carmen to tell her he was going home. Carmen immediately objected. She told him he needed to stay for graduation. Tomás told her that graduation ceremonies did not matter. He knew he had done well and had made the grades. He would get his certificate. He did not need to attend the graduation ceremonies. This broke Carmen's heart. She scraped together enough money to purchase the required white shirt. She must have discreetly talked to some others who admired Tomás' accomplishment. Two other Christians in the town, who remained anonymous, bought shoes, trousers, and socks. Tomás proudly attended his graduation ceremony.

Receiving the clothing shortly before graduation greatly impacted him. That was when he started to realize how great a God he had. Tomás felt he had the best uniform at graduation because it was all handed to him from God. At that time, he made a commitment to serve God as his life's calling.

Tomás had talked to me about the possibility of going to seminary. But he had no money and would not be able to purchase the warmer clothing he would need in Medellín. So he decided to serve God by teaching at a Christian day school in a village overrun with guerillas. During his three years in that village, God gave him the privilege of winning several of those children to the Lord. Occasionally, he returned to Magangué, so I was able to keep track of his maturing faith and his labor for the Lord. I would often say that God sent him carrying his bag of seed for sowing and reaping, and Tomás came back leaping for joy because of what the Lord had done.

A Men for Missions work team was volunteering at the Magangué dorm during one of Tomás' visits to help the dorm parents, which he did whenever possible. Tomás praised God and witnessed about how God was working in his life.

God laid Tomás on the heart of one of the men on the MFM team. John Schultz approached me and asked about Tomás' interest in seminary. I was glad to tell him that Tomás had been a terrific teacher and had a deep love for the Lord. I enthusiastically told John how God had performed a miracle to make it possible for Tomás to get an education and serve the Lord. Tomás was not one to take advantage of a situation. He was grateful and worked hard when given a chance.

John asked what it would cost to pay for Tomás to live at the dorm and to fund his seminary studies in Medellín. I did not know exactly, but I was willing to find the information. John made the commitment to be responsible for finding support for Tomás' four years of study at seminary.

Tomás arrived at the OMS-related Bible seminary in Medellín excited about the chance the Lord was giving him. It was an entirely new environment for him. He was a poor rural boy in the big city for the first time. But he was a humble person and was dedicated to his studies and to serving God. When I attended his graduation four years later, I nearly broke into tears not only because Tomás was such an outstanding student and received special recognition for his academic achievement while attending the seminary, but also for his devotion to Christ, his fellow classmates, and his professors. He had been attending classes with people who were college graduates while he only had a rural high school education.

Today, Tomás serves the Lord in a powerful way. He is a pastor in one of the church organizations OMS started in Colombia, the Inter-American Church Association. It goes against conventional wisdom that someone of his caliber would have his background. He is one of those rural Colombian treasures.

The youth from the river areas were hungry for an education, and they were hungry to learn more about Jesus Christ. Often they were driven by a strong desire to learn more so they could help other members of their families and communities. This desire was what my fellow missionaries and I were seeking. We knew it was so much more effective to take a felt need and use it to spread the Gospel. Evangelism is most effective when people of a nation are trained to evangelize their own communities. The people in the rural areas may be poor and considered underprivileged, but they are precious. My fellow missionaries and I experienced the most joy when we witnessed nationals evangelizing nationals.

*****

Millie's insight: You cannot go into those rural areas where Christians are and not find those hidden treasures. You could go down those rivers and say, "Here again is another jewel. Here again is another. Here again is another treasure."

CHAPTER TWENTY-EIGHT

Present Your Requests to God

"So Peter was kept in prison, but the church was
earnestly praying to God for him." Acts 12:5

*****

Millie's insight: As we cast our burdens upon him, he will give
us rest and peace.

*****

I was overwhelmed. After Vernon's passing, God granted us
much success with our little schools. Vernon had planted spiritual seeds in the areas where our schools were increasing. Now
we were tilling the soil by opening little schools at an amazing
rate. It became impossible for me to visit all of the schools, the
office work was overwhelming, and I needed help with the
schooling of our two small girls.

I regularly shared praises and concerns with OMS mission
leaders. I expressed my need for someone to take over much of
the visitation to the schools because I just could not continue to
do all of the required work. They approached the national
church, which OMS had helped to create as the official organi-
zational structure for the jurisdiction of the churches being
established. The national church also ran the Christian schools.

For many years, I worked as the director for these Christians schools.

The national church leadership understood the need and saw an opportunity to spread God's Word. Luis Garavito, a young lay pastor, came to their attention as a possible candidate. He had traveled those rivers as a young boy with his father. Luis knew the river villages up and down the river. He could operate those little outboard motor boats with ease. The small congregation Luis pastored was stable. Several of the laymen had taken some of the ministry courses we offered and would be able to take over the pulpit while Luis traveled.

After meeting and praying for the selection, the national church leaders in Medellín felt Luis was the one they should contact. In their letter to his church and him, they requested that Luis be released one week every two months to travel to the river schools for me. He would oversee the writing of letters by the children to their sponsors, make the biannual reports on the children required by Compassion International, deliver student uniforms to the schools, take gifts to the children, distribute school supplies and teacher salaries, and encourage the teachers. My heart felt a little lighter as I returned to Magangué.

Getting the letter to Luis was another challenge. No postal service existed to the little river towns. I started a vigil, watching to see if anyone from his church in Colorado came to Magangué to conduct some business. I knew that was the only way I had of getting this crucial letter to him.

One morning, around 11:00, the doorbell rang. It was Luis. His dear congregation in Colorado had not yet been able to send someone to Magangué to visit me and extend their sympathy about Vernon's death. After a joyful greeting and expression of consolation, Luis related that his church had finished a night of prayer at 5:00 that very morning. They had received word of Vernon's death and knew it would affect the schools, so they gathered for an all-night prayer vigil. They were seeking God's direction, as they wanted to help with the ministry of the little schools.

These dear believers knew the load I was carrying; however, they knew nothing about the letter from the national church.

During the wee hours of the morning, they voted to release Luis two weeks every two months to do the required traveling to keep the little schools supplied and flourishing.

God had answered my need by doubling the release time the national church had requested. God's church was praying, and he answered abundantly. But we still had one more urgent, essential request—a Colombian Christian who was prepared to take over the coordination of the schools. We started praying.

When Isidro Rojas entered the Peniel Bible Institute some years before, he was not one you would have thought would finish as an outstanding student in his class. But he did. After successfully serving as a teacher in the river area schools, he returned to Peniel Bible Institute as a teacher. Later, he studied for a year in the Medellín Bible Seminary.

Isidro did not feel called to be a pastor, but he had a sincere desire to serve God in our schools in rural Colombia. He longed to see God work in the schools, in the homes of the children, and in the churches in rural villages. He testified that he had found his place in the harvest field and experienced great joy when he was serving God there. I had moved to Medellín, so a person to take over the school supervision was needed. The national church chose him to take my place as coordinator of the Christian day schools.

I transferred all the responsibility of record keeping and distribution for the Christian day school program to Isidro. When requests were made for children to be sponsored with Compassion International, they were assigned a number that included the number of the school in their village. The history of the children—including age, grade, who the child lived with, and a photograph—was all documented. Compassion required that an update be made on each child every two years. The biannual reports documented the children's physical welfare and school progress. Children were required to write three to four letters a year to their sponsor. The sponsors could also write letters to their students. Those letters were translated upon arrival at their country's Compassion International office. Addresses were not given to the students or sponsors to prevent inappropriate contacts or solicitation for more funds.

We had not sent anyone to check on the school in Plan de Armas (the area where Vernon had his accident) in more than a year. The need to get the new biannuals, to take new case histories, and to check the financial books in the school there was becoming a concern.

Early on a Thursday morning, Isidro left Medellín for the three-day trip to Plan de Armas to visit the school. He had boarded a train for Puerto Berrio. He would then ride the bus to Landazuri, where believers from the Plan de Armas church would be waiting to accompany him the rest of the way. He was carrying funds from Compassion International for the school, which included each child's monthly amount to help with tuition, as these were private schools. He also had materials to collect the needed data on the school and children it served. On Friday evening, around 9:30, I received an anonymous phone call. I was asked a series of questions about Isidro Rojas and his purpose for going into Plan de Armas.

Immediately, I knew I must be very careful answering the questions. During the first few seconds of that call, I calmed myself as I prayed, "Lord, may I be able to say the right thing at the right time and keep all data clear." It was obvious that Isidro was in serious trouble. Guerrilla activity had become more intense during the past few months in that area of Colombia. However, some of our national workers had gone into the area during Easter week. They had been stopped, searched, and questioned by the military about their reasons for traveling into the area, but that was all. Their trip had been uneventful. Had the region become more dangerous?

I was in anguish that night and the next couple of days. What was happening to Isidro? Had he been kidnapped? Had he been robbed and then killed? I prayed repeatedly for his safety. I shared my concern for Isidro with three other missionary couples and asked them to pray for him. The professors of the seminary held a special time of prayer on Saturday morning, but they were careful to not reveal too much as we had no more information than the mysterious phone call. I carried on my normal daily tasks to help shield my tremendous burden from the children, but at the same time I involved them in praying for Isidro's trip to the little school.

On Sunday morning, I knew that I was going to see his wife Doña Alba and their two darling children at church. Did I dare share my concern with them? What could I tell them? I asked God for wisdom and prayed during the church service, *Lord, bring Isidro safely back to this lovely family.* I still did not feel free to share that mysterious phone call with Doña Alba. I would have to trust God to answer my pray for his safe return.

As I was putting the finishing touches on lunch for my family, I stopped to pray, *Lord, the burden is so heavy. Please give me peace about Isidro.* Around 2:30 that afternoon, I thought, *I must not rest until I have spent some more time in prayer for Isidro.* When I started to pray this time, the burden was gone. It was as though the Lord gave complete assurance that Isidro was out of danger. I did not know if this meant that he had been released from the enemy or if God had taken him to his heavenly home. Either way, I felt complete peace.

Just before 6:00 that evening, someone knocked at my door. The children rushed to greet our visitor. When I opened the door, the children enthusiastically yelled, "Isidro, Isidro!" What an answer to prayer!

Isidro related what had happened before he continued traveling home to his family. The bus had been about halfway to Landazuri when it came to a Colombian army checkpoint established because of recent violence. They uncovered that Isidro was not from the area and asked where he was going. When Isidro said he was going to Plan de Armas, they were suspicious about his reason for traveling into that region. When they searched his belongings, they discovered he had papers with English headings, the children's letters with North American names and Colombian names, photos, a camera, pesos worth about US$600, and other items that indicated his work with foreigners. He was incarcerated.

At about 12:30 p.m. on Friday in the military jail, he was questioned. Who was he working for? What was his purpose for being in the area? What was he going to do in Plan de Armas? They demanded a phone number. By that time, the

OMS office was closed for the weekend. The only other number he had was mine. He would discover later that God had given him the right words to say, but at that moment, this fact was not evident as he was placed in a cell with 10 prisoners from Plan de Armas.

All of his belongings, papers, and money were taken from him before he was placed in the filthy cell. The night was miserable. Mosquitos and bugs were rampant, the cement floor was cold, and he had no coat or cover. What he did have was a captive audience. Isidro did not waste the God-given opportunity; he witnessed to his fellow inmates. One of the men asked for pointers as to how to study the Bible. He owned a Bible but laid it aside because he did not understand how to study it. Because Isidro had been stripped of everything except his clothing, he had no way to write down instructions so he promised to send some information when he returned to Medellín.

Isidro was hopeful Saturday morning. Surely by that time they would have made contact with me to confirm he was not a threat, but no one even talked with him about why he had been jailed. He was sent out on a work detail with the other prisoners. Saturday night he questioned one of the prison workers. He was given no information so he settled in for another night in jail.

Up until that point, Isidro hoped that the letters and other belongings would be returned to him in a timely manner. He would then continue to Plan de Armas. But now, disappointment set in as he realized it was too late to even think about completing his trip. Even if he were released, the people who were to escort him on the last part of the trip would no longer be waiting. It would not be safe for him to attempt traveling there alone.

On Sunday morning, the colonel ordered the other prisoners out to work, but Isidro was told he was going to the dungeon. What did that mean?

After the others had left for the day's work duty, he was informed that they had talked with his company leader and satisfactory answers were given. I found it interesting to know they thought I was his company leader. But more important was the fact that Isidro and I had been able to give the exact information as to what he was doing without giving information that might have placed him under more scrutiny in that dangerous situation.

At 8:30 on Sunday morning, Isidro was released from jail. Only God knows why they had not released him Friday night immediately after talking with me. God may have been protecting him from another more dangerous situation. By 2:30 Sunday afternoon, he was back in safe territory. We praised God.

*****

Millie's insight: God promises to provide for all our needs. He has already chosen the people who will fulfill those needs.

CHAPTER TWENTY-NINE

Not in Vain

"How, then, can they call on the one they have not believed in? And how can they believe in the one of whom they have not heard? And how can they hear without someone preaching to them? And how can they preach unless they are sent? As it is written, 'How beautiful are the feet of those who bring good news!'" Romans 10:14–15

*****

Millie's insight: Many of our workers today are people who came to know the Lord through their teachers in our primary Christian day schools.

*****

With great anticipation, I made preparations to speak at a Christian women's conference being held in Montecristo. I worked for days, preparing material, and I had made provisions for someone to care for my teenage son Howard.

I enjoyed visiting Montecristo, a village on the Nechí River with a population of about 600. It is in an area of Colombia, with beautiful landscapes. But my favorite sight was the pristine, picturesque lake that greeted me just before arriving in Montecristo. I advised and encouraged the teacher in the Christian day school during my visits. Because I felt safe in this area, I had even brought my children with me on visits in the past.

Three days before I was to leave, I received a phone call from an area that was close to Montecristo. They stated that they were calling for the Montecristo church. This shocked me. I did not realize that it was possible for a telephone call to be completed from such a rural area to the city of Bogotá where I was living. However, it only took a moment for me to recover from my surprise. I exclaimed enthusiastically, "I am all ready to come."

The caller responded by saying, "I have called to tell you not to come." The caller went on to explain that the Christian workers in Montecristo had recently been visited three different times by guerillas. The first time, they demanded to know the source of the money that paid the teachers' salaries. The teachers responded that the children paid a small fee. This was true. The children did pay a very small fee—if they could. By that time, Compassion International was helping OMS fund tuition for many children. The teachers that were confronted by the guerrillas received part of their salaries from those funds. But the teachers were very careful to not mention Compassion International at all.

The second time the guerillas went to the school, they wanted to know who provided the school supplies. How did they get them? The teachers said they received them from different places. They were vague and tried to cover it over. As part of Compassion International's program, OMS was allowed a certain amount of money per student to purchase supplies and uniforms for students. Gifts to the OMS school ministry were also used to supply the schools. Actually, the children had very few individual school supplies. The OMS missionaries were very resourceful at using the children's tuition money to purchase the basic supplies they needed. Each student would have a couple of notebooks and a pencil or two. The only reading books in the school had to be shared. For example, there may be three first grade reading textbooks in the school, and all the first grade children read from them.

During the third visit, the guerillas wanted to know when the foreign lady was coming back. That was when the leaders of the church in Montecristo decided to send word to me that I should not come. It was obvious that it would not be safe for me to visit, nor would it be safe for them to have me amongst them. This took place during a time when Colombia was said to have 85 percent of all the kidnapped people in the world.

When I was told it was too dangerous for me to travel to Montecristo, I was extremely disappointed. It wasn't that I had spent a great deal of time preparing for the visit—even though I had. It was the fact that I could not visit my dear Christian friends until things quieted down, and I knew that might take a long time. I was strongly connected with the Christians in Montecristo. Those believers had a strong, vibrant relationship with Jesus Christ. The little Christian day school was providing a primary education for the village's children. I enjoyed visiting that little village school and encouraging its teacher.

Montecristo developed into an area that attracted displaced rural people. These people left their homes because of the guerilla activity around their farms. The guerillas lived in the jungles in the southern regions of the state of Bolívar. They went to the rural farming regions and ordered those hard-working farmers to give them this, this, and this or they would kill the farmers. In many places, entire families and villages were massacred. When the guerillas came, people fled to safety with whatever they could quickly grab and carry.

Because of the senseless violence inflicted by the guerillas, the people of Montecristo petitioned the government to provide protection for them. But no protection came. Finally, a desperate group of men decided to go to Bogotá and confront the government officials in person. They walked for miles and miles. When they reached Bogotá, they visited the government offices. But that was not the only place they wanted to visit. They wanted to see me. All they knew was that I worked at the Inter-American Christian School. They asked directions and found the school.

When those simple farmers in their farm clothes arrived at the school and asked to see me, the principal told them that I was not in town and would not be returning soon. They left a message and sadly departed. It was impossible for the principal to determine if they were honest people with good intentions. At that time, I really was on a trip to the northern regions of Colombia. I was saddened to learn that I had missed seeing my friends. For when I heard the names and descriptions of the farmers, I recognized them as believers. However, I must admit that the principal probably would not have allowed me to greet my friends because of the danger of a possible kidnapping. We had no recent contact with Montecristo and the area was volatile, so the threat to my safety would not have been worth the risk.

Because of the issue of the displaced people putting a strain on the existing services in Montecristo, Compassion International had partnered with OMS there. Eventually this project helped about 300 children at a time. Compassion International supplied the resources for part of the teacher's salary, children's school uniforms, and some school supplies. However, in 2005, the area became so dangerous that not even the Colombian national workers from Bogotá could safely travel to that area. Because of their inability to monitor the use of funds, Compassion International decided to discontinue the project at Montecristo and focus their efforts on the displaced rural people who had found their way into the large metropolitan areas. The refugees were humble farm people who knew how to produce food and build simple homes, but they had no skills for navigating the challenges of survival in the city. These people needed much help because they had no idea how to handle city life.

Even though I was not able to visit Montecristo again, after I retired from serving Jesus as a resident missionary in Colombia, I received a DVD from Luis Carlos—one of my former students from Montecristo. The DVD was really a video letter of thanks to me for my efforts to bring God's Word to the village of Montecristo and the surrounding areas. It had background music proclaiming how important it is to bring the love of Jesus to the 40 percent of the people in the world who have not heard the Gospel, many of whom have not even had an opportunity to learn to read. It proclaims that these people in the mountains, along remote rivers, and in the deserts are forgotten by church organizations as they argue about this thing and that thing. The message of that song is that Christians must not close their hearts because there is so much need. The music and the message of that song are powerful and convicting. It beautifully states that God's church must be a light in the darkness. The pictures on the DVD were taken in the region around Montecristo. Luis Carlos's love for the area where he grew up is evident through the way he portrayed those vibrant people.

The DVD ends with a letter to me from Luis and his sister

Aminta. They expressed their thanks to the Christian teachers who taught them in their little village and for the fond memories they had of their experiences while living in the Christian dorm and attending high school in Magangué. They expressed gratitude to me because of the impact my ministry had not only on them, but also many of their family members, friends, and acquaintances. They stated that they often heard about me and how I was responsible for helping to bring the Gospel to Montecristo and other areas where suffering was widespread and the Gospel of Jesus is unknown. They state that their education was a result of the work of OMS through Compassion International. They were grateful.

Aminta returned to Montecristo after graduation from our Christian high school in Magangué. She began working with the Compassion International project in her own hometown. Before long, she was administrating the Compassion International part of the project in that rural area. However, in 2005 she received notification that Compassion International was planning to close the project because of the danger that outsiders faced when visiting the village.

Aminta and Luis tried for two years to convince Compassion International to not close their program in the Montecristo area. They knew the good that was being done for their people and feared what would happen to the children if outside assistance stopped. It was inevitable. In April 2007, the leadership in Bogotá explained to Aminta that the focus of their work was changing to meeting the enormous needs in the cities instead of the rural areas. Even though I am sad about that decision, I understood because of the number of kidnappings that were occurring.

Aminta and Luis were crushed. They, along with some of the other young people who had received Christian training and education through the work of Compassion International, said they would not let God's work stop. In the meantime, Aminta had been able to receive training to be a health administrator, which is somewhat equivalent to that of a licensed practical nurse in the United States. This allowed her to manage the health program in her rural community. Not only was she working to ensure the children had an opportunity for Christian education, but she was also working to provide her people with health care. Since Compassion International would no longer provide funds for local projects, those vital services would end.

These dedicated young Christian adults and their Christian friends decided to start a foundation to fund their work with the children. They realized they had to continue the program for the Christian education and care of the poor children. They named the foundation Vidas del Sur (Lives in the South). They knocked on doors and talked with everyone they could think of so the children in their remote area could be educated and learn about Jesus. Their work is now the only relief effort to combat the violence, the conflict, and the problem of the subsistence living in their area of the country. They simply could not let the fact that they were no longer going to receive aide be the reason that the children of their humble country people would feel the consequence of hunger due to crops being destroyed by floods or by guerrillas on a rampage. The children must not be left out. People must understand that there is a real need in the department (state) of Bolívar.

Aminta and Luis are relying on God to provide his wisdom and to show them how to continue the work through their foundation Vidas del Sur. This foundation is now supplying food, clothing, and a Christian education for about 300 children. In the name of Jesus, Aminta and Luis hope to lift the children out of the extreme poverty in which they are living.

Because of my deep love for the people of Montecristo and the humble rural Colombian people, I cannot watch the video made by Luis and Aminta without tears filling my eyes.

*****

Millie's insight: God's work will continue as long as believers are discipled and trained to continue evangelizing. God's Word will not return in vain.

Epilogue

Other than a few months here and there for deputation in the United States, I lived continuously in Colombia during most of my adult life. I did spend three years in the late 1980s in the United States when Colleen and Joyce entered college. They had been educated in Colombia with the exception of one year while they were in grade school during a home ministry assignment in the United States. I felt I needed to be close by for the first year or so of their college education to help them make a smooth transition into life in the States.

During the first year of that stay, I was just Mom. I did not travel. We lived in Wilmore, Kentucky, and I worked on Christian education projects in Spanish on the elementary and junior level for our Colombian churches. The last two years included quite a bit of traveling as I raised funds and accepted speaking engagements. After that time, I felt both Coleen and Joyce were comfortable living in the U.S., so Howard and I returned December 31, 1989, to my beloved Colombia and my missionary family.

Over the years, I had often said I did not want to be sent to Bogotá because, at an elevation of 9,000 feet, it was too cold there. Yet, I spent the next 13 years living there.

When Howard was ready to attend college in August of 1992, I only stayed in the States for three months because it hadn't been that long since he had lived in the U.S. On this trip, I attended some meetings, visited family and friends, and settled Howard into college.

People started asking me if I would return to Colombia each time I planned a trip to the United States. I had turned 60, so they assumed I was making retirement plans and would stay in the States. Each time retirement was mentioned, I replied, "I have no reason to retire as there is still work to do for the Lord in Colombia. How are these people going to get the light if I decide it is time for me to rest?" Did people not understand God's Word does not mention retiring from his work at a certain age?

The new OMS field leader was Randy Spacht. Randy had

217

called before he accepted the responsibility of field leader to ask me to be his assistant field leader. I had great respect for Randy, so I accepted even though it did mean I would have to move to Bogotá. Most of the official mission business was done there because that is where the government offices are located. Actually, I felt it would be a tragedy for Randy to leave Medellín because he was one of the most outstanding professors at our Bible seminary. God had given him such a tremendous gift for teaching.

Randy was a joy to have as a supervisor. He often said, "I carry the title of Colombia field leader, but Millie does the work." What neither he nor I realized was that he was training me to be a future field leader.

Most of my mission work in Colombia was with children and training adults to work with them. I saw the need for the development of programs to reach the children. Actually, the assistant field director position gave me precious time to train workers for children's Christian education. What a blessing to have an opportunity to use my gift for working with children. I designed the programs to train adults how to win children to Christ, how to disciple children, how to plan and direct VBS, how to plan and conduct children's camps, and many other types of children's programs. These programs were successful. Before long, I was able to start training Colombian nationals to take over the responsibility of leading the children's programs.

During the first years I was stationed in Bogotá, one of our churches in the southern part of the city gave me a small storage area. It was actually just a hole in the wall at the entrance of the church. Nevertheless, it was a location to store my materials. The entrance to that tiny space was so small that I was about the only person who could go into it to retrieve or store materials.

After about four years, the children's outreach had grown so much that we were in desperate need of materials. I wrote to the churches in the U.S. who supported me and asked for unused Sunday school or VBS materials. They responded by sending down barrels of materials. I used those materials to build up a library of resources for the Colombians to use.

By this time, my children's materials had outgrown the original small space at the entrance of the church. The church had purchased a building next to the Inter-American Christian School. They installed a door between the school and the church to make access between the buildings more convenient. I was given an apartment on the third floor of the church. This made it so much easier to adequately store the children's materials. Workers could easily see what was available and there was space for them to choose and prepare the materials.

I lived across the city from the church, and it was unsafe for anyone to be on the streets after 7:00 p.m. That third-story room was large enough for me to place a bed in there. This was a special blessing because it provided a place for me to spend the night if I did not finish my other duties before dark. I parked my car in the school patio area so it would also be protected. The school employed a watchman 24 hours a day. Later, an electrical alarm system was installed, and a watchman was only employed during the daylight hours. We were in the middle of an area where guerrillas and drug lords operated. Violence and terrorist activities were prevalent.

In the 1990s, the field office was constantly updating our evacuation plans as the conditions were constantly changing. We never knew if we might have to suddenly evacuate our missionaries and their families from Colombia. Some mission organizations did withdraw their personnel during this time. OMS gave each missionary the opportunity to leave, but after fervent prayer and careful managing, all chose not to leave due to the guerrilla and drug lord activity.

In 1999, I was named field leader for OMS Colombia. This meant that OMS' missionaries in Colombia had suggested me as a possible candidate for the position. After prayer and careful consideration, one or two candidates were recommended to OMS headquarters. The OMS Board made the final selection. The field leader serves a four-year term.

As field leader, my major responsibilities included making sure the needs of the missionaries were met, maintaining a good relationship with the national church, and conducting the official business of OMS in Colombia. I was a member of the national church committees as an advisor and observer as they moved out from under OMS supervision. Colombians were ready to start running their own church. The people in leadership were strong believers and well trained.

In the 1980s, OMS had turned over ownership of all properties to the national church because of the situation in China when the communists had taken over the government. When OMS had to leave China years earlier, the properties were left without an owner so the government confiscated the properties. In an effort to prevent the same thing happening in Colombia, the national church board was given ownership of the OMS properties, as we did not know if we would have to suddenly leave the country if violence became too severe. This was the start of turning over responsibility for the maintaining of property and programs to the Colombians.

The time from the early 1990s through 2003 was a very difficult period in Colombia. During those years, 85 percent of all kidnappings in the whole world took place in Colombia. While I served as field leader, one of my responsibilities was to monitor the movements of missionaries to make sure they were not taking unnecessary risks.

We did not have cell phones until a couple came down to minister to our missionaries at the annual OMS conference. This dear couple was attacked right in front of my apartment. She was shot in both hands. I accompanied her to the hospital where she stayed for a week. When she returned to the States, she required several surgeries and almost lost one hand. Because of the sudden attack, her husband had an immediate issue with his blood pressure and was taken to the emergency room. After this, it was decided all adult OMS missionaries should have cell phones for security purposes.

After that incident, a good share of our communication about our movements was in code. This presented a problem because it was difficult to communicate the code—especially to the OMS office in the states. We had no idea when our written communication would be intercepted. For that reason, people traveling from one area to another were used to communicate the current code. The code was to let our people know when we left one area of the city and when we reached at our destination. That way they would know when to expect us and when we had arrived safely.

I might tell my secretary that I was going out to get some bananas. This meant I was going to Libertadores, which is an area in southern Bogotá where we had a church and a school. Later I would call and tell her the bananas were beautiful which meant all was well there.

In 2002, we started the process of turning all the business operations of the mission over to the national church. Mature, equipped Colombian Christians were ready to assume the work. It was during this time that Randy Spacht approached me about my plans for retiring. At that time, he was serving as international regional director for the OMS work in Latin American. His home base was in the United States, but he often traveled to Latin American countries.

I could not bear the thought. Just thinking about leaving my beloved Colombia and my many dear friends was almost too much for me to bear. I had been a missionary for 49 years, and I could not see myself in any other role. I even asked Randy to not talk with me about it because I knew I would cry. I had already cried many tears in private as I thought about what I knew was inevitably coming.

In April 2003, Randy again approached me with a proposal. I would move to the United States but would return to Colombia a couple of times a year as long as I was able to do so. I looked at him and said, "That might work. How soon may I come back?"

Actually, I had been hatching a plan. I was thinking of getting my things ready, taking a taxi to the airport, and quietly leaving. I knew I would not be able to say goodbye in person.

Arrangements were made for me to leave in August. Randy suggested I return to Colombia in late November for our high school graduation ceremonies. That was perfect. I said, "*Hasta luego*," which is Spanish for "I'll see you later."

Since my official retirement from full-time missionary work, I have returned to Colombia two to four times a year and staying one to four weeks. The length of time I stay depends on the type of work I do while I am there. I have led an average of two Men for Missions teams each year.

My mission activities are not confined to leading short-term missions teams to Colombia. I also continue to raise funds for our Christian schools, for scholarships for needy students, and for money to assist seminary students.

Throughout my life, my God has protected me in many dangerous situations. When I was approached by friends and even family about whether or not I would return to Colombia during some of those dangerous periods, I replied, "I'd rather be in Colombia in God's will than in the safest place in the U.S. outside of God's will."

> When that work is all completed,
>   He will gently call you home;
> Oh, the rapture of the meeting!
>   Oh, the joy to see you come![8]

*****

Millie's insight: Some people feel if they have a leadership position they have been lifted up. I never felt that way. I am too simple. The glory is all God's.

Endnotes

[1] Mrs. Charles E. Cowman, *Streams in the Desert* (Los Angeles: The Oriental Mission Society, 1941), 11.

[2] Composer unknown, "With Christ in the Vessel," Traditional chorus, http://www.klangwesley.com/songs.php?songID=52

[3] Anna L. Coghill, "Work, for the Night Is Coming," 1854, http://cyberhymnal.org/htm/w/o/workfort.htm

[4] William and Gloria Gaither, "The Family of God," 1970, http://www.musicnotes.com/sheetmusic/mtdFPE.asp?ppn=MN0066368&

[5] Cowman, 42.

[6] Cowman, 43.

[7] Author unknown, "Safely Home," (Sacramento: American Tract Society).

[8] Author unknown, "Safely Home," (Sacramento: American Tract Society).